G000046893

'Dramatic. Lively. Well-informed. Pe[...] Bible story is different from many [...] whether used as a script for public p[...] its vitality will engage. You'll learn [...] individual stories, their setting and the big story all at the same time. I enjoyed reading this book and I'm sure you will too.'

Derek Tidball, Evangelical Alliance, Prolific Author,
Former Principal of London School of Theology
Former President of the Baptist Union

'As a published author I know how hard it is to come up with an original approach to well-handled material. But Pete Atkinson has done it! This is an imaginative and novel approach to the greatest story ever told that will captivate those unfamiliar with its subject matter, and educate those who thought they were. It is a very unusual creative work - I've not come across anything like it before. I love the insights and connectivity of threads across scripture, and I commend it to your attention.'

Pete Gilbert, Author of 'Kiss and Tell' (2003, CWR)

'"The Rescue Mission" by Pete Atkinson is a fresh, imaginative, dramatic and partly poetic presentation of the Biblical account of the history of mankind and God's love. It is very creative while remaining loyal to the meaning of the Biblical text. The energy and emotion of this book can bring the reader into a greater love for God.'

Ellis Potter, L'Abri, Author and Pastor

'Pete Atkinson has provided an invaluable tool in the wide perspective overview of the Bible. It will undoubtedly be an attractive read for those who as yet have no faith at all and are just interested.'

Ranald Macaulay, Author of 'Being Human' (1998, IVP),
Son-in-law of Francis Schaeffer

30130503271825

The Rescue Mission

Pete Atkinson

THE BIBLE AS A GRIPPING, THRILLING, EMOTIONAL PAGE-TURNER

ISBN 978-1-291-20446-9

The Rescue Mission

Pete Atkinson

For Bethany

0.00 - Order to Chaos

Tears cascade incessantly from the blood-shot, pain stained eyes of three friends huddled together. Mourning their loss, with arms wrapped around each other, all cry out in agony.

Together this intimate embrace forms a creative community of love called Elohim, where joy and affection find their home. If only the trio had maintained all their focus within their embracing circle of paradise, there would be no tears falling today. But Love by its very nature looks outward. And the view breaks Elohim's heart.

Everywhere hatred glares back.

Everywhere suffering permeates.

Everywhere every thought is evil.

Holding hands tight, faces flooded with tears, hearts *filled with pain* (Gen. 6:6), Elohim grieves. Hope has died. Their nature - their community of paradise - is incompatible with the torture-scarred landscape. There can be no relationship.

With the outlook so bleak, Love is left with only one option.

Gripping each other ever closer, the three whisper their united conclusion, '*I will destroy all human beings that I made on the earth...*'

The voices break down, choking and trembling under the weight of emotion. The sounds of sobbing, the manifestation of a deep inner distress, are eventually accompanied by further strained words.

'*...because I am sorry I have made them* (Gen. 6:7).'

The decision is definite.

Elohim has chosen.

Humans will suffer no more.

Because all humans will be destroyed.

Mourning their loss, tears fall like raindrops, flooding the entire earth.

The devastating conclusion couldn't be more different from the one originally dreamt of, envisioned, and sculpted by Elohim.

In the beginning (Gen. 1:1), out of love, passion and desire for relationship, the heavens and the earth took form in spectacular fashion, bringing order to chaos. The three friends leapt enthusiastically. '*Let us* make *human beings in our image and likeness* (Gen. 1:26),' they cheered, overjoyed at the prospect of sharing their nature with the centrepiece of their creation. Having provided for their every need, the breath of Elohim rushed through man and woman, releasing life.

Everywhere Elohim looked, the complete work of art shone with excellence (Gen. 1:31). The Artists smiled expansively with the utmost pride and satisfaction.

Full of joy, there was no pain.

Full of love, there was no shame.

Full of life, there was no death.

Of all the great gifts showered upon the first humans, the greatest was freedom. Free to roam and explore however they wished, the possibilities were endless. And the most incredible opportunity of all was to spend time in the company of their Creator, to live in intimacy with the Breath that brought them life. Created by Love, for love, to love, the relationship would fulfil the deepest desires of Elohim's heart.

But relationships can never be forced.

Love must be freely chosen.

Love must be freely reciprocated.

And the Artists could not have presented the reality of humanity's choice more clearly: *in the middle of the garden were the tree of life and the tree of the knowledge of good and evil* (Gen. 2:9*)

'*You may eat the fruit from any tree,*' Love explained. '*But you must not eat the fruit from the tree which gives the knowledge of good and evil. If you ever eat fruit from that tree, you will die! (Gen. 2:16-17)*'

Two trees: one brought life, the other brought death.

And the three friends of Elohim held hands in eager anticipation, dreaming of - and longing for - the affections of their delicately crafted masterpieces. Vulnerable, with heart fully flung out on the line, Love could do no more than cry out 'Choose life!' and watch on transfixed, waiting for response.

Mouths dropped in shock and horror.

When, into the scene, doubt descended.

From order to chaos, clarity was distorted.

From the tree of knowledge, fruit was selected.

And from each eye the first tear of rejection fell.

Having chosen disconnection from their Designer, human elegance diminished. Full of shame, man and woman no longer fully reflected Elohim's community of total joy.

The human image was scarred.

Yet still succulent fruit hung from the tree of life, ripe for picking.

Still humans could choose to eat the fruit and *live forever* (Gen. 3:22). But full of shame, they would have been wounded forever. Forever they would have fallen short of their originally intended beauty. From this there could have been no turning back.

The prospect was terrifying.

Acting quickly to avert an eternal catastrophe, from which there could have been no rescue, Elohim forced man and woman out from the garden and erected a spectacular security barrier *flashing back and forth to guard the way to the tree of life* (Gen. 3:24*).

Far from home, having never previously worked to survive, the daily necessities of life became a constant challenge for the first humans. Within a generation, frustration fed jealousy and anger.

Then murder.

Spilt blood cried out from the ground (Gen. 4:10), contaminating the Artists' lush handiwork, staining and stifling, rendering it no longer fertile for crops.

'In an attempt to end the bloodshed and the spiral of decline,' a voice from within the intimate embrace of Elohim recalls, 'I told the first murderer, Cain, "*If anyone kills you, I will punish that person seven times more* (Gen. 4:15)." I hoped the warning would discourage revenge attacks. But, with my words again abused, revenge spread instead like a contagious disease. Within five generations, Lamech, a descendant of Cain, boasted arrogantly, "*I killed a man for wounding me, a young man for hitting me. If Cain's killer is punished seven times, then Lamech's killer will be punished seventy seven times* (Gen. 4:24)."'

With a hint of optimism, another voice of Elohim sighs, 'I dream of one day teaching humans to forgive not *seven times, but seventy seven times* (Matt. 18:22).'

'But I can live in humans no longer,' a third voice interjects, heartbroken. 'The extremity of human dirt has smothered all beauty, making us incompatible. My breath will leave their flesh and *they will live only one hundred and twenty years* (Gen. 6:3).'

Death.

Death has arrived.

Mourning their loss, tears fall like raindrops flooding the entire earth.

0.01 - We Choose To Enter

For as long as we can remember getting behind these walls has been the epitome of impossibility.

Today the gates are open.

Many times before we have walked past this rundown, dilapidated building and looked back with disdain, relieved to live in a new, more aware, more advanced era. This throwback to an ancient way of life had simply left a scar on today's landscape.

But occasionally - just occasionally - the dull, discoloured concrete and smashed windows have appealed to our inquisitive nature. Every now and again, we have stopped to wonder whether this derelict eyesore contained any discarded treasures.

And today, it's as if the building is ushering us in.

We enter not knowing what to expect.

We lay down all preconceptions, all prior knowledge.

We choose to enter with an open mind.

Inside the building, our heart thumps as we clamber through the debris spread chaotically across the floor. Occasionally we stop to inspect objects of interest - before a door in the distance catches our eye. It is rugged and stripped down, in keeping with the surroundings. Sunbeams reflect off a silver, metallic plaque, drilled onto the door.

Engraved into the plaque are the words: 'Rescue Headquarters.'

Our heart skips a beat.

Captivated by intrigue, we push open the door.

'Are we ready to do this?' a voice from Elohim asks.

'Love is always a risk and we love too much not to,' another responds. 'Love always opens itself up to the possibility of rejection. It's the only way. But the agony of heartbreak will be worth it for the joy of acceptance, the ecstasy of relationship.'

'Just look at Noah's beauty,' adds a third besotted voice. 'Suffering may saturate every life but this is not a lost cause. Our character has not disappeared completely. In Noah there is hope. In Noah there is inspiration (Gen. 6:8-9).'

'Starting with Noah our character can spread out across the globe, overwhelming all hatred. Love can win out.'

'Humans can be beautiful again. Restored to full splendour, they could once again access the tree of life. They could be eternally attractive.'

'Remember how incredible it was walking with the first humans through the garden. Our relationship together can be even more intimate than that!'

'Oh, it will be glorious. I cannot contain my anticipation. My heart leaps with excitement.' The voice pauses, taking a deep breath. 'I would be willing to die for that.'

'So we are agreed then?'

'Yes.'

'Yes, let's do it.'

'Let the Rescue Mission begin.'

PHASE ONE

1.01 - A New Beginning

With just one foot inside the room we are instantly amazed. Besides bookshelves and a desk, this is no ordinary office. Every square inch of the room's four walls is decorated with paper and card, all filled with detailed text, diagrams and illustrations.

Mesmerised we don't even notice the door close behind us. Instead we rock back on our heels, and look up then down, left then right, in an attempt to take it all in. The extent of the information is simply overwhelming. Of one thing we are sure: this 'Headquarters' must be the hub of a substantial, strategic operation.

But before the prospect of having stumbled upon the secret lair of a criminal gang truly materialises in our thoughts, we are gripped by text to our left, on the posters nearest to the entrance. Beneath the prominent heading, 'Phase One,' a mysterious narrative begins:

From the sanctuary of her undercover decking, Noah's wife stands watching the downpour drive down and bounce high off the bobbing surface. Looking out over the waters she picks out a single carcass from the masses below. Is this mutilated mess the remains of a human? It is too difficult to tell now.

Every night Noah's wife is haunted by the shrieks, the final cries of the massacred. For forty days now she has been haunted by the images: friends and strangers alike flung through the air, flailing, gasping, pulled under, never to be seen again. They didn't stand a chance. *Even the highest mountains* were submerged (Gen. 7:19).

If only.

If only.

If only they'd listened to Noah. His ship was more than big enough to save them.

Every night she weeps, grieves, overwhelmed by the devastation.

For most the torment would paralyse both their body and mind.

But not this courageous woman.

This woman feels privileged.

Precious.

Significant.

She is the mother of the only family left alive.

Every new sunrise, Noah's wife is motivated on by a bright, burning love for her three sons, their wives, and of course Noah, her brave yet tender hero. Though he had appeared insane, though he was abused and humiliated, supporting her man on his mission was the best decision she ever made. Without his expert craftsmanship this remarkable woman would not be here now. She would be adding negligible weight to the mass of meat and bones being tossed about by the waves, rotting before her very eyes.

Her skin crawling, Noah's wife is lost in a haze of thoughts when her husband's shout reverberates through the ship.

'It's stopped! It's stopped!'

Her head jolts.

Could it be true?

The eyes focus.

A myriad of circles no longer dance across the rocking waves.

Vertical streaks no longer flash furiously.

She holds out a hand.

The palm returns dry.

A skip, a hop, a dance, her sprint has it all. Arms flinging chaotically, she runs like one of her ship's galloping creatures, head first into the hysterical embrace of her family.

'*Grow in number and fill the earth* (Gen. 9:1),' Elohim cheers as every creature required for creation's fresh start steps back onto dry land.

It's the second time that creation has heard this command to create. Despite the disastrous results last time, Love has given humanity a second chance to thrive.

But the same dilemma remains: love cannot be forced. To love or to hate, to nurture the Creator's image or to stifle it, that remains the choice of humans.

'*I will demand the life of anyone who takes another person's life* (Gen. 9:5),' Elohim tells Noah, desperate to cut down the disproportionate revenge attacks which last time spiralled out of control and became a precedent.

Violence is still a distinct possibility.

God may one day be grieved to the point of destruction again.

Which prompts his first covenant.

A promise.

An agreement.

A contract.

This covenant with the whole world will place a marker in the ground, signposting a critical, irreversible choice. The decision will stand firm and true throughout the entire Rescue Mission.

With great passion, Elohim announces to Noah, *'I now establish my covenant with you and with your descendants after you... never again will there be a flood to destroy the earth... I have set my rainbow in the clouds, and it will be the sign of the covenant between me and the earth* (Gen. 9:9-13*).'

The promise is unconditional. Even if humans choose to tarnish themselves just as severely as they did before, even if every thought becomes evil again, Love will not give up. God is in this for the long haul, fully committed to fulfilling the vision of his Rescue Mission. No matter the cost.

The promise is unreserved. In no disillusionment as to the scale of the challenge, knowing only too well that *their thoughts are evil even when they are young* (Gen. 8:21), the Creator has chosen to never stop believing in the fundamental goodness of his artwork. This is a new beginning, and God has faith that his beauty will ultimately win out.

Noah lies naked, drunk out of his mind. The next morning, still hung over, the one man worth saving fires a curse upon his grandson Canaan, staining his descendants for generations to come.

For beauty and love to reign, the Rescue Mission certainly has a long way to go.

PHASE TWO

2.01 - We Will Birth

Three friends look down upon a large chart, full of painted text, arrows and illustrations. Each face portrays deep thought and concentration.

'Let's review this again,' a voice breaks the silence. 'Our rapidly multiplying population has divided into various nations. With so many different languages, confusions and divisions fuel violence and tension.'

'So here's the plan,' another voice continues. 'We will birth our own nation, *to live right and be fair* (Gen. 18:19), to promote our values.'

'It will be great and highly respected across the earth,' adds a third voice. 'All nations will see our love and be attracted.'

'By blessing our nation all *the people on earth will be blessed* (Gen. 12:3).'

'And they shall own the land currently inhabited by the people Noah cursed, the Canaanites. That way our blessing shall overcome the curse.'

'But to be Love to all nations, our nation will have to choose it first. Like Noah building his ship, our plans require co-operation.'

'*Should I tell* Abram *what I am doing now?* (Gen. 18:17) I wonder, Abba, how will he respond?'

In complete unison, the Community of Elohim lean forward, and paint five letters in vibrant gold: 'FAITH.' Abram will respond with faith.

A frustrated kick to the ground sends a cloud of dust puffing up into Abram's face. The wanderer shakes his head, flicking dirt back into the air. Where did it all go wrong, he wonders?

Though he is *rich in cattle, silver and gold* (Gen. 13:2), here in the land of Canaan, Abram feels far from satisfied. Drought after drought, famine after famine, Abram has to continually move on in search of fertile land. The nomadic existence is worlds apart from the prosperity he previously enjoyed in the great secure city of Ur.

Desperate to clear his jumbled mind, Abram walks aimlessly, dragging his feet through the hostile sands. Nearly a decade has passed since he heard the promises that brought him to Canaan (Gen. 12:1).

But a decade on, nothing has changed. Not one promise has materialised. Abram has absolutely nothing to show for his faith and trust.

'*Look all around you,*' God told Abram recently. '*All this land that you see I will give to you and your descendants* (Gen. 13:14-15).'

The voice was just too definite and powerful to doubt.

Yet the very mention of descendants made Abram feel sick.

Sarai, his wife, is unable *to have children* (Gen. 11:30).

She is permanently infertile.

And in a society where family ties bring status, the shame is relentless. For decades now, Abram and Sarai have fought their grief, finding comfort in each other, coming to terms with their tragic, irreparable void. Elohim's recent promises had simply opened the wounds again.

With evening drawing in, Abram arrives home to find his tent empty. Exhausted, he falls to the ground in a crumpled heap.

'*Abram, don't be afraid.*'

Digging his head further into bent knees, Abram strains to stifle a tired, aggravated groan.

'Abram, *I will defend you, and I will give you a great reward* (Gen. 15:1).'

The voice belongs to Elohim.

With tears welling in his eyes, his cheeks burning, Abram can hold it in no longer. The question which incessantly pounds within is finally let fly.

'God, *what can you give me? I have no son, so my slave... will get everything I own after I die* (Gen. 15:2).'

'*You will have a son of your own* (Gen. 15:4).'

God's adamant tone carries with it great tenderness. It soothes Abram's anger.

Guiding Abram outside, Elohim invites him to stare into extensive depths, far into majestic star-filled sky.

'*There are so many stars you cannot count them,*' Elohim explains. '*Your descendants also will be too many to count* (Gen. 15:5).'

Slowly but surely Abram's cheeks lighten. A satisfied smile stretches wide. The awesome sight is evidence enough for Abram. He is convinced: the Architect of all this beauty is surely capable of blessing him with a child (Gen. 15:6).

'Abram, Abram, where are you?'

Abram freezes. Sarai is home: what should he say?

'I'm out here, my love.'

Feeling his wife's arms squeezing round his waist, playfully swaying him from side to side, feeling her great affection, tears begin to roll down Abram's cheek.

'What is it, love?' Sarai whispers, stroking her fingers reassuringly through his hair. 'You can tell me.'

Abram turns to look far into his wife's eyes. 'God met me again. I will... I will be a father.'

Sarai looks away, humiliation hanging from her face.

'God *has kept me from having children* (Gen. 16:2*).'

Sharing her pain, Abram embraces his wife.

'I know, I know.'

Clearing away the teardrops from her blurred vision, Sarai looks up again into Abram's eyes. Though each word hurts considerably, she speaks with clarity: *'Go, sleep with my maidservant; perhaps I can build a family through her* (Gen. 16:2*).'

2.02 - Out of Love

The discomfort in our gut is sharp.

God wants his nation to demonstrate love.

Surely he wants it to be born out of love, doesn't he?

Not a one-night stand.

'Abram believed God,' the text on the wall says. *'And that faith made him acceptable to God (Gen. 15:6).'*

It all seems absurd.

How is this faith?

How is Abram sleeping with Sarai's maidservant, faith?!

Alongside the written narratives, there are hundreds of interweaving arrows, jottings and sketches, forming an intricate, complex web. Some markings have been written in paint and pen. Others have been written in pencil. Others have been crossed out. Some pencil markings have been traced over in pen.

To what extent, we wonder, will things happen as the Rescue Strategists intend, as they desire?

Abram can sleep with Sarai.

Or Abram can sleep with Sarai's servant.

The choice is his.

Love can instruct.

Love can inspire.

Love can woo.

But Love cannot - Love will not - control.

In pencil, our eyes glimpse the name 'Ishmael': the name of Abram's child born of Hagar, Sarai's maidservant (Gen. 16:4). *Abram,* the wall tells us, *was eighty six years old when Hagar gave birth to Ishmael* (Gen. 16:15).

Though no one is around to hear it, we immediately regret the laughter which slips out. But then again, why shouldn't we laugh? Fathering a child at the age of eighty-six: that's just insane. No wonder Sarai doubts her capability to conceive.

Maybe, Sarai's unsatisfactory solution really was the only option available.

At least Abram is a father now, as promised.
This will have to do, we reluctantly concede.

As Ishmael grows, Love watches on with the infatuation of a devoted father. By the time Ishmael reaches the age of thirteen, the Community of Elohim are so enthralled by their precious, maturing creation, they choose to declare again, and cement forever, their commitment to Abram's family. To mark the occasion of Ishmael's coming of age the Rescue Strategists choose to unveil a second covenant - another crucial, future defining moment.

So important, so foundational, the event must never be forgotten.

Which is why, from now on, Abram will be known as Abraham.

The new name means 'father of many.'

'*I will be your God and the God of all your descendants*' (Gen. 17:7), Elohim promises, his voice full of pride and excitement.

Abraham's family shall be God's family.

Elohim shall be their Father, the father of many.

He shall nurture, mature; draw out their beauty.

Into the contract, a condition for relationship is written. Under the agreement, every male belonging to Elohim must be cut by a knife, marked by circumcision, as a constant, physical reminder of where the whole community's identity lies - a constant reminder of how precious, how treasured every child of God is.

Sure enough we locate the covenant promises on the charts pinned to the wall. In amongst the pencil jottings, these words stand out; for they are written in indelible ink.

An intimate relationship begins.

And God's commitment is definite.

With great pride, Abraham watches his son playing boisterously in the distance. Ishmael has grown into a strong young man. Though he certainly has a wild streak, Abraham can still picture his son enjoying relationship with Elohim, absorbing God's great character, basking in his covenant.

At last Abraham can relax and rest, secure in the knowledge that he has left a tremendous legacy.

With a smile on his face, Abraham closes his eyes.

'*I will change the name of Sarai, your wife, to Sarah* (Gen. 17:15).'

Abraham's eyes open, surprised and alert.

'*I will bless her,*' Elohim continues, '*and give her a son, and you will be the father* (Gen. 17:16).'

As if tripped by a wire, Abraham's knees buckle forward and his face crashes into the dust. The very words he's longed to hear all his life: at first a burst of ecstasy fills his stomach then his laughter slows, the sound nervous and disturbing. He trembles with fear. The terror is devastating: Sarah is simply too old to have a child; even if she did conceive she would surely die in labour.

With his teeth clenched and eyes screwed tight, Abraham's gasp is almost inaudible: '*Can a man have a child when he is one hundred? Can Sarah give birth... when she is ninety?* (Gen. 17:17) *Please let Ishmael be the son you promised* (Gen. 17:18).'

'*No, Sarah will have a son* (Gen. 17:19). *I will establish my covenant with him* (Gen. 17:19*).'

Nursing his exhausted wife, Abraham places an arm around Sarah's shoulders. Leaning forward he softly kisses her forehead.

Feeling her husband's touch, Sarah opens her eyes and smiles. '*God has made me laugh,*' she says, looking down at the miracle babe asleep in her arms. '*Everyone who hears about this will laugh with me* (Gen. 21:6).'

'We shall name him after our laughter,' Abraham adds, placing his thumb through his son's tiny fingers. 'You are important and precious to God, Isaac.'

'*Abraham!*' God calls out. 'Take Isaac, *the son you love, and go to the land of Moriah. Kill him there and offer him as a burnt offering* (Gen. 22:1-2).'

Abraham sets off, without question. By now, he trusts every word God says.

After three days travel, father and son reach their mountainous destination.

An altar of wood is prepared.

Onto which Isaac is tied down.

Isaac: Abraham's precious, promised son.

Inheritor of a prosperous future.

Born miraculously.
Out of love.
Abraham sharpens his blade.

Sweat forms on our brow.
How could Love possibly want this?
Has God given up?

The knife draws back, rising high over Isaac, poised to strike a deathly blow.

2.03 - Collision is Coming

Ever since the horror of the Phase One floods, a deep-rooted anxiety has ricocheted within every human. All are acutely aware that their life hangs in a delicate balance, dependent on the behaviour of forces from the sky, forces beyond human control.

Too much rain, all life is submerged.

Too little rain, all life soon withers.

Hijacked by fear, all stare to the heavens in desperation. This isn't how it should be; something has gone dreadfully wrong. The outside forces, assigned some form of personality, must be furious. To somehow calm the anger, humans decide to offer gifts. And as desperation persists, offerings become increasingly extreme.

Some fathers even offer the greatest sacrifice of all.

They kill their firstborn child.

The knife draws back, rising high over Isaac, poised to strike a deathly blow. Unable to look, Abraham turns over his shoulder. Eyes clenched tight, his heart pounds furiously, pain pulsating through his being.

'Abraham! Abraham!'

His knife still airborne, the father freezes.

'Don't kill your son or hurt him in any way (Gen. 22:11-12).'

Ever so slowly the words soak in. The left eye opens first, then the right. His muscles relax. His racing heart slows. And as if in slow motion, Abraham's raised arm drops safely to his side. He falls to his knees, and wraps himself tight around Isaac's distressed, shaking frame.

Relieved beyond measure, tears surge.

After what seems an age, Abraham looks up to see a ram caught in a thorny mountain bush.

'You are surely precious and loved,' Abraham whispers into his son's ear, 'the ram shall take your place.'

Unified in their pain, united in their resolve, the Community of Elohim look into each other's eyes. In the most dramatic way possible, they have made their point. The creator and controller of the elements does not demand human sacrifices. Love shudders at the sight of spilt human blood. The killing of innocent children leaves Love totally repulsed.

'Oh, Abraham, precious Abraham, he has such beautiful faith. Even before tying up Isaac, he told his son, '"*God himself will provide the lamb for the burnt offering* (Gen. 22:8*)."'

'Yes, we will. His words reach out to the very core of our Rescue Mission.'

'In the same locality as Abraham's offering, we will provide.'

'My father will offer the greatest sacrifice of all.'

All day Jacob anxiously pushes onwards, moving fast, desperate to put ground between himself and his enraged pursuer. Focussed as he is, running for his life, Jacob hardly notices the setting sun until darkness has engulfed and he can go on no further. Drained of all energies, gasping for breath, the runaway is forced to rest.

In all his life Jacob has rarely ventured far from the family tents. Tonight he will sleep homeless and alone. A quiet introvert, Jacob has never wanted to cause much fuss. But after what he has just done, he is unlikely to ever return home in peace.

What is wrong with me, Jacob cries? How could I trick my father like that? What had he done to deserve that?

Ever since his near-death experience as a child, Jacob's father Isaac, has lived with 'God will provide' engrained in his psyche. When his beautiful wife, Rebekah, was unable to have children, Isaac had reason to believe that God could - and would - provide.

Rebekah gave birth to twins.

One she named Esau.

The other: Jacob.

The miracle of two sons took Isaac by surprise.

The blessing was magnificent.

But it was also problematic.

Only one of his sons could inherit God's covenant inaugurated with Abraham. Having left the womb first, this privilege was Esau's. Esau's descendants would be as many as the dust of the earth.

Jacob shudders. Cold and afraid, the runaway rests his head on a stone and falls fast asleep, his mind seamlessly slipping into a curious alternate reality.

In his dream, Jacob sees *a ladder resting on the earth and reaching up into heaven* (Gen. 28:12). *'I am* Yahweh,' cries a voice above the ladder, *'the God of Abraham your grandfather* (Gen. 28:13).'

The image is revolutionary. Most humans believe that the 'powers' on which they depend for life, are elsewhere, external, disconnected. But this ladder in Jacob's dream actually connects heaven, the home of a divine power, with the earth. And far from being cold and distant, this 'force' interacts personally, using the name Yahweh.

'Your descendants,' Yahweh continues, *'will be as many as the dust of the earth. All the families of the earth will be blessed through you and your descendants. I am with you and will protect you wherever you go* (Gen. 28:15).'

We stop in our tracks. This isn't right.

Esau is the oldest son.

God's covenant will continue with Esau, not Jacob.

Why is the Rescue Strategist conversing with Jacob?

Why is he promising Jacob as many descendants as dust on the earth?

Jacob wakes to eerie silence, and in a flash, haunting memories flood his mind's eye. He recalls Esau, drawn and bedraggled, *almost dead from hunger* (Gen. 25:32), looking him in the eye and begging for food. And all Jacob saw was an opportunity. In exchange for a bowl of soup, Jacob demanded, *'You must sell me your rights as the firstborn son* (Gen. 25:31).'

So selfish.

So heartless.

Then there's the con which fooled his father.

The con which roused his brother's vow to kill (Gen. 27:41).

For the rest of the night, Jacob stares out at the stars, wrestling with his shame. As the hours pass, Yahweh's promises gradually take root within him, enabling a healthy combination of confidence and humility to flourish. *'I want God to be with me and to protect me,'* Jacob declares as a new day dawns. *'I want to return in peace to my father's house* (Gen. 28:20-21).'

But no amount of regret, no amount of remorse, can change the past. The reality remains: Esau is still out for his blood.

Two decades later, Jacob looks on in terror.
An army four hundred strong is heading straight towards him.
And leading the march is Esau.
Jacob gulps, draws breath and steps forward.
Today Esau shall have his revenge.
Jacob falls flat on the ground, lying completely exposed.
He peers up.
Esau is running right at him.
Collision is coming.

2.04 - Father's Arms

Arms wrap around.

Braced for pain, instead a delicate kiss impacts Jacob.

Overcome, surprised to be locked in a forgiveness filled embrace, tears tumble. *'It is like seeing the face of God,'* Jacob tells his brother, digging deep to find the right words, *'because you have accepted me* (Gen. 33:10).'

Spontaneously swinging their arms in elation, three friends jump ecstatically, linking hands in an explosion of celebration, forming a community of Love called Elohim. Together they dance in majestic unison.

'Yes, yes, it's happening!' each sings in beautifully diverse tones, joining together in stunning harmony. 'Our image spreads, our love unites, our forgiveness restores.'

'I'm creating some stories,' a spoken voice explains, 'to encapsulate our Rescue aspirations. I want everyone to know that my Father's arms are outstretched. One story begins with a son rejecting his father's affection. And in Jacob and Esau's embrace I have found the climax: *While he was still a long way off,* the *father saw* his son *and was filled with compassion for him.* So *he ran to his son, threw his arms around him and kissed him* (Luke 15:20*).'

'That is brilliant.'

'Son, it is beautiful.'

Wallowing in depression, a long drawn out groan leaves Jacob's mouth, matching the volume of his rumbling, empty stomach. The remarkable reconciliation with Esau, over two decades ago, was the last time Jacob truly felt joy. Since then tragedy after tragedy have shattered his heart.

Sometimes numb and empty, sometimes throbbing and sore, today's pain finds its root in times of great joy long ago, in the days when Jacob learnt to love. It was when he fell head-over-heels for Rachel, a young woman of stunning beauty, that Jacob quickly learnt the extent to which love requires sweat and sacrifice. He had to toil for many years before finally marrying the love of his life.

And despite the great pleasures of partnership, married life was far from harmonious bliss for Jacob. Like his father and grandfather before him, his wife couldn't conceive. Knowing that his offspring would inherit astounding promises, Jacob chose instead to father ten sons with three separate women.

Each birth was simply wonderful, but then came a day like no other, one so, so beautiful. By repeating his exploits in the lives of Sarah and Rebekah, the Community of Elohim ensured Phase Two would continue in a lineage of love. Rachel gave birth to Joseph.

Jacob's miracle son.

A gift from God.

Born of his one true love.

Which is why, when Esau's merciful arms later wrapped around, Jacob couldn't have been happier with life. After all the mistakes he had made, he felt abundantly blessed.

That was before the first tragedy struck.

Bringing life to her second child, Rachel didn't make it.

The pain was too much.

She died in labour.

Then came further devastation.

Aged seventeen, Joseph was out shepherding the flocks.

When a creature savagely attacked.

Mauling Joseph to pieces.

And as if that wasn't enough, now Jacob's family is engulfed by famine. Far and wide, all face starvation. Catastrophe is imminent. Soon the descendants of Abraham, the foundations of the Rescue Mission, will be no more.

Only one hope remains. Rumour has it that out in the west the respected Egyptians have built up healthy grain reserves, and they are now selling their abundance of produce to travellers from around the earth. So Jacob has sent ten of his sons off on a mission to Egypt; his entire family's future dependent on their success.

Jacob turns to face his youngest son, the one he kept behind. Such a precious, precious sight, Benjamin is to be protected at all costs. Benjamin is the last remaining legacy of Rachel's love. And in his son's warm eyes, Jacob sees Rachel's relentless compassion.

And Joseph's steadfast confidence.

Benjamin's hands stroke back and forth on his frail father's shoulders, soothing another grating howl. Comforted, Jacob sits back, closes his eyes and offers up a silent prayer. Like he has done so many times before, Jacob tries to picture what Joseph would look like, all these years on. Having never found or buried his son's mutilated body, oh how he longs for a shred of fiction in the account of Joseph's death.

Holding hands, the three friends of Elohim lean forward in anticipation as ten of Jacob's sons stand in line waiting to purchase grain from an Egyptian governor. Inspired by passionate love for the governor, the trio have been waiting a long time for this moment. Over the last decade, they have been helping this governor oversee the stockpiling of Egypt's reserves, single-handedly saving countless lives.

The Egyptian governor has thrived in his rescuing role because he knows what it is like to have nothing. At a young age he was sold to Egypt as a slave. Then he was falsely accused of rape and thrown into prison. But his life took a turn for the better when he was asked to interpret the king of Egypt's dreams. Thanks to his revelation that fat cows represent an abundant feast of food, the prisoner received a position of respect, the king's own royal ring, and *fine linen clothes* (Gen. 41:42).

The storyteller in Elohim smiles, before continuing with a tale of a poverty-stricken son returning home. "'*Hurry!*' the father shouts, arms still tightly embracing his son. "*Bring the best clothes and put them on my son. Put a ring on his finger... get a fat calf and kill it so we can have a feast and celebrate. My son was dead, but now he is alive* (Luke 15:22-24).'"

The three friends of Elohim edge further forward, ready to jump in jubilant celebration as Jacob's ten sons reach the front of the queue and bow down in front of the kind-hearted governor. The trio's excitement is immeasurable; another extraordinary family reunion is imminent.

The governor is Joseph.

Jacob's Joseph: the firstborn of Rachel.

With his brothers knelt down before him, Joseph has here a remarkable opportunity. Because the lost son wants nothing more than to rest once again in his father's arms. And to hear him celebrate, '*My son was dead, but now he is alive.*'

2.05 - They Face Execution

Despite the most unquenchable desire to see his father, the sight of his ten brothers causes every emotion of Joseph to be hijacked by anger. It's like his eyes catch fire as fury explodes.

'You are spies! (Gen. 42:9)' Joseph bellows, pointing his finger furiously.

A deathly silence falls. All in the bustling marketplace are stunned.

Shivers shoot down the brothers' spines. Aghast at the allegation, their frantic protests fall on deaf ears. The ten are dragged away under arrest, bewildered and petrified, oblivious to the proximity of their long lost sibling.

Joseph sits dead still, locked in rage; poised to lash out like a wounded animal. With every eye on him, the governor just wishes the ground would swallow him up. He bites his lip, desperate to maintain dignity. But inside, the throbbing pains of age-old wounds pulse through every fibre of his being. His mind plays through the events which cut his wounds raw: the day when he was stripped naked, dragged across dirt, hurled down a well and traded into slavery.

By his own brothers.

His own jealousy fuelled brothers.

Embarrassed, Joseph rises to his feet and walks sheepishly through the speechless crowds.

Stripped.

Dragged.

Hurled.

Traded.

Deeply suppressed bitterness and fear is excavated as the memory plays over and over. But another image niggles away, that of his aging father desperate for food.

Joseph is a man torn to the core. Pulled apart by hatred and love he wrestles a longing to rescue against a lust for revenge.

After three days of strenuous deliberation, Joseph settles upon a compromise. He decides to grant freedom and food to all but one brother: Simeon will remain imprisoned. This way, those freed will have reason to return to Egypt, keeping open the possibility of reconciliation.

What's more, to increase the likelihood of return, Joseph lays down an ultimatum. *'Bring your youngest brother back here to me,'* he demands, *'if you do this... you will not die (Gen. 42:20).'*

Before long the sacks of grain from Egypt are empty.

To live the brothers must return.

And without Benjamin, they face execution.

'Everything is against me (Gen. 42:36),' Jacob sighs. *'I will not allow Benjamin to go with you. He is the only son left from my wife Rachel.* If anything happened to him *I would be sad until the day I die (Gen. 42:38).'*

Every brother can see their father's distress. If only they could just come clean about selling Joseph into slavery, they would end so much of his pain. Judah falls to his knees and takes hold of his father's dry, wrinkled hand.

But no confession leaves his lips.

'Send Benjamin with me,' Judah proposes. *'I will guarantee you that he will be safe, and I will be personally responsible for him (Gen. 43:8-9).'*

Their eyes locked, Judah sees far into his father's agony.

Head in hands and shoulders slumped, Jacob slowly nods.

He has no choice but to trust Judah's word.

As the frail father sits pale faced, drawn and motionless, seemingly stripped of all emotion, he hardly notices his sons' tender kisses goodbye. All afternoon and evening, Jacob stares straight-ahead, eyes fixed on the point where Benjamin disappeared from sight. Alone, with no energy to move, only now do tears drip from his chin one by one.

Why God, why?

Why be so cruel?

Cutting the back of his throat, an infuriated cry slices the cool night sky.

The sense of déjà vu is not lost on Jacob's sons. They are once again under arrest, standing fearfully before the same Egyptian governor. The only difference this time is the prosecution has plenty of evidence. Benjamin was caught red-handed, caught stealing a valuable royal cup.

But Benjamin is completely innocent.

And the governor knows it: it is he, Joseph, who has set him up. Joseph has meticulously manufactured the scenario so that Rachel's second son shares the same fate as her first: imprisonment and slavery.

As *powerful as the king of Egypt* (Gen. 44:18), Joseph can lay down his revenge in an instant.

How will his brothers respond to Benjamin's plight?

Have they changed?

Or are they still riddled with selfishness, only caring about themselves?

Judah steps forward, his vow to protect Benjamin swirling in his stomach. *'Master, what can we say? How can we show we are not guilty?* (Gen. 44:16)'

Joseph sidesteps the question. *'The man who stole the cup will be my slave. The rest of you may go back safely to your father* (Gen. 44:17).'

Picturing his father's agony, picturing Jacob's unending misery, Judah clutches his chest and rips his clothes. *'Please allow me to stay here and be your slave. Let the young boy go back home with his brothers. I cannot go back to my father if the boy is not with me. I cannot stand to see my father that sad* (Gen. 44:33-34).'

Joseph stares transfixed, not quite believing his eyes. Judah is a man totally transformed from the brother he once knew.

Sacrifice has replaced selfishness.

Empathy has replaced jealousy.

Compassion has replaced hatred.

Joseph can control himself no longer. The respected ruler breaks down, weeping inconsolably, as over a decade of pent up emotion breaks free.

'I am...'

Brushing away tears, Joseph looks up into his brothers' frightened eyes.

'I am Joseph. Is my father still alive? (Gen. 45:3)'

In the past, Judah would have hated the sight of Joseph and Benjamin hugging. The two golden boys together again, the favourite sons of Jacob, just the thought of it would have made Judah feel sick.

But today, a great liberated smile fills his cheeks. Judah was the catalyst of this reunion and he is a changed man because of it. Not since childhood has joy felt like this.

Judah has learnt that actions are most powerful when they are sacrificial. In the Rescue Mission, progress is made when individuals offer themselves in place of others.

2.06 - Completing Phase Two

'Joseph is alive.'

Lost in heavy slumber, Jacob groans.

'Joseph is alive.'

Jacob's head rocks fiercely, chaotically, as if tortured by a dream.

'Joseph is alive.'

The voice is getting louder, clearer. And somewhere in the sleeper's consciousness he registers hands holding - shaking - his shoulders. Slowly Jacob opens his eyes. There in front is Benjamin, grinning wildly.

'Joseph is alive.'

One after another Jacob's sons squeeze their father's fragile frame. In the glorious hubbub, the warmth of each hug rouses Jacob's senses, waking him fully to the world.

In the embrace of Simeon, free from Egyptian prison, long lost remnants of joy are resurrected in Jacob's heart. He even manages a laugh. And it is here, in the arms of his lost son, that the words finally strike home: Joseph is alive!

Urgently, desperately, Jacob looks around.

One, two, three, four… eleven.

'Joseph is alive,' Benjamin repeats again, eyes resonating with conviction. His father looks around again, not knowing what to think. Each son fidgets with such genuine excitement, perhaps it is true; perhaps Joseph is alive. Jacob chooses to take hold of a fragment of hope.

'Joseph is still alive,' says Judah, jumping on the spot, 'and he is *ruler over all the land of Egypt* (Gen. 45:26).'

Jacob's heart sinks like a rock. His eyes roll, turning to the heavens in disgust. My own sons, why do they lie? Joseph: ruler in Egypt? Why be so far-fetched? Do they think I'm stupid?

Benjamin takes his father gently by the hand.

'Let me show you something. Then you will know it is true.'

Reluctantly Jacob nods.

He follows Benjamin outside.

Where several majestic wooden wagons stand.

Egyptian wooden wagons.

'The king of Egypt gave these to us because Joseph is highly respected.'

Jacob stands rigid, not knowing whether to laugh or cry. Over the passing minutes he becomes increasingly mesmerised. A warm flow of love gushes through Jacob's stomach, dissipating all aggravated tension, and before long, it's as if he were standing alone with Joseph. Moving with ease, Jacob draws beside the vehicles and places his palm on the wood.

Tenderly he strokes.

Now I believe you (Gen. 45:28). Gather everything together; we're moving to Egypt!'

Overjoyed by the sumptuous spectacle, in the Community of Elohim the Father reaches for his Son's hands, opens up the palms, and tenderly strokes his Son's wrists. Their faces exude absolute, united determination.

Their Rescue Mission is underway.

They have laid the foundations.

Thanks to Joseph's lifesaving accomplishments, Abraham's descendants have not only survived imminent starvation but they will now experience affluence. In Egypt, Elohim's chosen children will be highly respected. '*I will give them the best land in Egypt* (Gen. 45:18),' the king has promised. '*Give them the best of what we have* (Gen. 45:20).'

And what most thrills Father and Son is Joseph's realisation of their intimacy, his recognition of their involvement in events. Oh, how they smiled when Joseph told his brothers, *'Don't be worried or angry with yourselves because you sold me here. God sent me here ahead of you to save people's lives* (Gen. 45:5).'

Anticipating the events about to unfold, a third figure joins Father and Son in intimate embrace and together they watch as Joseph rushes into the outstretched arms of his father, Jacob. Celebrating the spectacle, the trio experience pure joy. And when Joseph turns to his brothers with profound forgiveness shimmering from his eyes, euphoria reigns. The instant they hear Joseph declare that, '*God turned your evil into good* (Gen. 50:20),' hope soars in the embracing Elohim.

Because together, this community is Love.

And Love is transformation.

Love is turning filth into beauty.

Love is making all things new.

And at last, those who are loved so dearly are beginning to recognise the actions of Love.

Next on the wall we read that Jacob's name has changed to 'Israel.' Grasping how much God values transformation, we start to search for the significance of this change.

We step back to examine the entire wall containing both Phase One and Two and the first thing that strikes us is how cluttered and untidy everything appears. Across every generation, deceit and betrayal have ripped relationships apart. Yet, by drawing alongside individuals, the Rescue Strategists have successfully encouraged honesty and loyalty to triumph. And in the process the Rescue ambitions have progressed.

But Egypt, we remember, is not the land promised to Abraham. That land is still currently inhabited by the descendants Noah cursed: the Canaanites.

We turn through ninety degrees to face the wall adjacent. In a striking font at the top we read the heading, 'Phase Three.'

And below, painted in the middle of a giant map, there it is.

In large letters, the word 'Israel.'

The land on the map is called Israel.

And Israel is divided into twelve regions.

One is labelled, 'Judah.'

Another is called, 'Benjamin.'

The regions, we quickly conclude, are named after Israel's twelve sons.

'*I am about to die,*' Joseph tells his brothers, the sons of Israel. His voice may be frail with age but the brothers can sense no hint of sadness; just optimism and assurance. '*God will take care of you... He will lead you out of this land to the land he promised to Abraham, Isaac and Jacob* (Gen. 50:24).'

Ever since Joseph was sold into Egyptian slavery, he has never once stepped foot again in Canaan. He has never once returned home.

Before breathing his last, Joseph has one final request: '*Promise me that you will carry my bones with you out of Egypt* (Gen. 50:25).'

Joseph's body is mummified and laid to rest.

In a coffin.

In Egypt (Gen. 50:26).

Over four hundred years will pass before Joseph gets his dying wish. Not until the conclusion to Phase Three will Joseph finally return home (Josh. 24:32).

PHASE THREE

3.01 - Into the Wilderness

Responding to agonised cries, three friends traipse across arid desert. Pyramids may protrude the horizon but this group walks with heads bowed to the dusty ground. They are driven onwards by an epic united ambition. Together, they cross the barren wilderness in search of one man, one man to end oppression, to end all the suffering; one man to rescue.

In unison all three draw to a halt. The Father of the group reaches out his hand, and wipes away teardrops swept chaotically across his Son's face. The third friend takes both Father and Son by the hand and, looking far into their eyes, slowly whispers, 'We must keep going.'

Motivation found in each other's tender affection, the trio look back at their substantial progress. Together the Community of Elohim smile: the three have only left one trail of footprints in the sand.

Since the time of Joseph, the family of Israel has flourished. Still guests in Egypt, they could by now be a nation in their own right. After all, Egypt was only ever intended as a temporary home, precious respite en-route to a far greater destination. And with the food crisis long over, the Israelites could have left Egypt in pursuit of Yahweh's promised, covenanted land.

But God's promises were ignored.

The Israelites remained in Egypt.

And covenant progress stalled.

Firmly rooted in Egyptian culture is an awareness of dependence upon forces beyond human control. Over the nation's vast history, each external influence, assigned a name and appearance, has been promoted to the status of a 'god.' Throughout the land, numerous statues of manufactured deities are worshipped enthusiastically by thousands in search of survival, favour and prosperity.

Born to introduce the one true God to the whole world, Abraham's descendants need to be carefully nurtured. Only by promoting Yahweh's character will the established nation of Israel stand out from all others. To grow and mature, the chosen children must enjoy a close relationship with their Father.

But as generations pass, far from developing differences, the Israelites embed further into the fabric of Egyptian society.

Adopting their culture.

Adopting their ideals.

Adopting their gods.

Gifted the most privileged position on the planet - an opportunity to experience and know the real deal - the Israelites instead opt for counterfeits. Passionately absorbed by his children's movements, the insulting blows invoke jealousy in the Father's heart. Love shudders. Betrayed and rejected, the community of Elohim is forced out into the wilderness.

An arrow on the wall, points us back to an incident in Phase Two where, in a dark, terrifying nightmare, God revealed to Abram, *'Your descendants will be strangers and travel in a land they don't own. The people there will make them slaves and be cruel to them for four hundred years* (Gen. 15:13).'

And sure enough, at the beginning of Phase Three, *a new king, who* does *not know about Joseph, comes to power in Egypt* (Ex. 1:8); and he wastes no time in putting the booming Israelite population to work on his ambitious construction projects.

We rack our brain in distress.

Slavery for four hundred years: was this really God's plan, foretold long ago?

Was this really what God wanted to happen?

Or were God's words, simply a statement of what would happen?

Does Elohim have foresight into the future?

Or were God's words merely a prediction of what could happen?

Our brain hurting, we return to the Phase Three text.

The slave drivers show no mercy, demanding more and more.

Thrashing.

Beating.

Whipping them into action.

Respect has turned to contempt.

And the Israelites' opportunity to leave Egypt is no more.

Homing in on their man, the three desert explorers flinch as leather connects with Israelite skin, bruising and slicing. The short, sharp stinging sensations have now persisted, with ever increasing intensity, for over a century. Still in these early days of relationship, already the pain of the loved ones is shared by the Lover.

Oppression eventually escalates to sadistic proportions. To stifle the Israelite population, which would soon be large enough to revolt, the Egyptian king implements strict measures of birth control. *'Every time a boy is born,'* his legislation reads, *'you must throw him into the Nile River (Ex. 1:22).'*

Mourning the innocent screams of their drowning infants, Elohim's agony stokes furious flames of anger. By the Mount of Sinai, a thorn bush bursts into a ball of fire.

'Moses, Moses! (Ex. 3:4)'

A nearby shepherd staggers back, cowering in fright. The bush before him, on fire but not burning up, now calls his name. Dehydrated in the heat, Moses holds his head, gripping with tense, firm fingers.

'Do not come any closer,' warns the voice. *'Take off your sandals, because you are standing on holy ground. I am the God of your ancestors - the God of Abraham, the God of Isaac and the God of Jacob (Ex. 3:5).'*

Petrified, Moses covers his eyes. His chest contracts so tightly his whole body quivers.

Guilt overwhelms.

Because forty years ago Moses lashed out, striking a man to the ground.

And now he anticipates thunderous judgement.

'I have seen the troubles my people have suffered,' the God of Abraham continues. *'And I have heard their cries when the Egyptian slave masters hurt them. I am concerned about their pain, and I have come down to save them (Ex. 3:7).'*

Not just heartfelt, this voice is heartbroken. The raw emotion catches Moses completely by surprise.

'So now I am sending you to the king of Egypt. Go! Bring my people, the Israelites, out of Egypt! (Ex. 3:10)'

Forty years ago Moses' desire for liberation caught the Rescue Strategist's attention. Though his actions cannot be condoned, Yahweh knows that this man shares his burning rage. In the face of injustice they are both unable to look on and do nothing.

Opening his eyes, Moses' hand slides slowly down his face.

One question thumps within him.

How?

How?

How can Moses possibly confront the king?

Forty years ago he struck down an Egyptian slave driver.

And ever since, he has been fleeing those out for revenge.

Moses is a wanted man.

Wanted for murder.

Head bowed to the ground, buckled under the strain, Moses' question stutters and stumbles out, '*How can I?* (Ex. 3:11)'

Love's response is instant: '*I will be with you* (Ex. 3:12).'

3.02 - I Called My Son

His heart still racing, Moses returns home to the reassuring arms of his wife. Safe again, Moses doesn't let go. His mind is overwhelmed, overcome by yet another momentous twist in his already eventful life.

By Egyptian law, Moses should have been killed at birth. Born during a horrific time of massacre, where all Israelite baby boys were drowned, Moses was saved by the quick thinking of his mother. At three-months old, she placed her son in a basket - covered in tar *so that it would float* (Ex. 2:3) - and released Moses downstream; who no doubt passed countless innocent corpses in the depths below.

Interrupting the shuddering narrative, we find on the wall a note covering the next portion of text. Taped across its top edge, forming a makeshift hinge, the additional information switches the scene:

In the dead of night, a young couple flee on a donkey with babe in arms. Knowing an order to slaughter all young boys in their region is imminent, the family take refuge in Egypt. Their son escapes the bloodshed, unlike countless other young lives tragically cut short by human hand.

Eventually Mary and Joseph receive the news that all those trying to kill their child have died (Matt. 2:20). At last, it is safe to return home. Relieved that their ordeal is over, Mary holds her toddler's hand tight.

The teenager knows the importance of protecting her innocent infant. Her nation's entire hopes of liberation rest on the shoulders of her firstborn son.

Concluding the short account, we read: *All this happened to bring about what the Lord had said through the prophet: 'I called my son out of Egypt* (Matt. 2:15).'

Already recognising parallels between this child's escape from massacre and Moses' own experience, the repeating themes of 'liberation' and 'out of Egypt' intrigues us.

Who is this precious child, echoing Moses' mandate?

And does the text really mean, 'the Lord said, "I called my son"'?

Can this human child really be Yahweh's son?

Underneath the note attached to the wall, the Moses narrative continues.

And so do the parallels.

'*Go back to Egypt,*' Yahweh tells Moses. 'All those *who wanted to kill you are dead* (Ex. 4:19).' The reluctant revolutionary saddles his wife and children onto a donkey and begins his return to Egypt, no longer a wanted man. '*Say to the king,*' Yahweh instructs, running through the liberation plans one more time, '*this is what* Yahweh *says: Israel is my firstborn son*' (Ex. 4:22).'

In some mysterious way, we conclude, the people of Israel and the young child of Mary and Joseph seem to be connected, both being described as Yahweh's firstborn. From the developing drama so far we have come to understand that, in these cultures, firstborn sons are highly prized. Loved favourably, they are the choice inheritors.

Stepping back onto Egyptian soil for the first time in forty years, Moses brings breath-taking news. Crying out for rescue, no Israelite could have imagined the extent of his revelation. The compassionate care of Yahweh and his ambitious intentions go beyond even their wildest expectations (Ex. 4:31). Hailed as a hero, Moses' confidence is on the rise.

The shepherd draws a large intake of breath then sets off to challenge the king. With his shoulders raised and back straight, Moses strides purposefully, carefully constructing his opening gambit.

'*This is what* Yahweh*, the God of Israel, says,*' Moses begins authoritatively, '"*Let my people go* (Ex. 5:1)."'

Taken aback, Pharaoh pauses. He turns his head to one side, sizing Moses up before uttering with disdain, '*Who is* Yahweh? *Why should I obey him and let Israel go? I do not know* Yahweh *(Ex. 5:2).*'

It's the very arrogance of the name 'Yahweh' that aggravates Pharaoh. Not to mention, the ambiguity.

Indeed, the meaning is a mystery to Moses too. During his burning bush encounter, Moses had asked, 'What if the people ask for your name? *What should I tell them?* (Ex. 3:13)'

And the reply came, '*I AM WHO I AM. When you go to the people of Israel, tell them, "'I AM sent me to you (Ex. 3:14).'"*

I AM WHO I AM.

Or equally, I WILL BE WHO I WILL BE.

In the original language each meaning is encapsulated by the name, 'Yahweh.'

Motivated by mystery, we choose to grapple with this fresh revelation. While 'Elohim' refers to the Creator of it all, the ultimate creative force, there is nothing in this name to suggest that this force is personal, relational; that this Creator is Love. 'Yahweh,' on the other hand, is a personal, relational name. But what could the name mean?

'I am who I am' appears to indicate an indefinable, unchanging nature. And as we consider the context of love and relationships, we connect the fixed state of 'I am who I am' with a parent's permanent affection for their child. For many parents, emotions can fluctuate as circumstances change, from sheer joy to devastated heartbreak, but their dedicated love remains unswerving no matter what, always desiring the best for their child.

This fathering commitment of God, we recall, is currently a privilege exclusive to the Israelites. We can therefore appreciate the Pharaoh's reluctance to take orders from a force he has never even heard of. Used to a diet of deities that he can see and touch, the concept of an invisible divine power seems ludicrous.

Insulted by the audacity of Moses' demands, Pharaoh decides to humiliate his challenger. '*Make these people work harder,*' he snaps at his slave drivers.

Devastated, Moses falls to his knees and deflects his anger skyward. '*Lord, why have you brought this trouble on your people? (Ex. 5:22)*' he cries. '*You have done nothing to save them (Ex. 5:23).*'

Moses feels betrayed. Without support, his uprising has been a laughing stock. He has simply made the oppression worse.

No wonder the Israelites have turned on him.

No wonder they shout, '*May* Yahweh *punish you (Ex. 5:21).*'

But Moses has no justifiable reason to be angry with Yahweh. He has forgotten that Yahweh had actually predicted that the king would *not let the people go (Ex. 4:21).*

And to the refusal, Yahweh had even provided a threat to counter with: *'Israel is my firstborn son,'* Moses was meant to have declared. *'You refused to let Israel go, so I will kill your firstborn son* (Ex. 4:22).'

Because, after the unremorseful drowning of Yahweh's own babies, justice will be done.

3.03 - And Kiss

'I will free you by my great power (Ex. 6:6),' Yahweh promises Moses. *'I will make you my own people, and I will be your God. You will know that I am* Yahweh *your God, the One who saves (Ex. 6:7).'*

The claims are astounding but Moses can only shake his head in bewilderment.

Why would anyone be concerned for the Israelites?

Resigned to a future of toil, the Israelites have given up.

Why would anyone want to save them?

Yahweh's apparent affection just doesn't make sense.

The Israelites have done nothing to deserve it.

In fact, they have done everything not to deserve it.

This is the god they rejected and consigned to history.

Egyptian powers are the here and now.

No credible deity would align himself with slaves.

The gods favour Pharaoh, for indeed Pharaoh is a god.

'I will punish Egypt with my great power...' Moses trembles as Yahweh's words reverberate through his body. With agony and fury, desire and longing, Yahweh declares war on Egypt's invented imitation gods. *'...Then they will know that I am* Yahweh (Ex. 7:5).'

The River Nile turns to blood, killing all aquatic life.

At the resting place of the Israelites' murdered infants, retribution begins. Yahweh strikes at the moment of the Nile god Hapi's greatest annual achievement, when the banks overflow and fertilise the land. But this year's flooding will contaminate all crops, and thoroughly humiliate Hapi.

Up from the river bound multitudes of frogs.

Annually increasing in number after the flooding, until now frogs have been a symbol of prosperity in Egypt. Even the goddess Heqet takes the form of a frog. But the extremity of this year's population surge makes Heqet an absolute nuisance. No Egyptian home escapes from a nauseating insurgence.

Drawn to the repulsive aura, gnats throng the air.

So far Pharaoh's magicians have successfully imitated both the blood and frogs phenomena, undermining Yahweh's credibility. But this time they have no such success. The magicians are forced to acknowledge the superiority of their nemesis.

In the gnats wake, swarms of flies descend.

To the Egyptians complete and utter disbelief, every single Israelite home escapes infestation. Yahweh promised to *'make a distinction between my people and your people* (Ex. 8:23*).' And he has. No longer in the realms of sorcery, this is miraculous.

Overnight, all Egyptian livestock is decimated.

Integral to Egypt's economic prosperity, many of the nation's gods, such as Hathor and Apis, take the physical form of cattle. But in one fell swoop Yahweh has undeniably humiliated these powers. And once again, all Israelite resources are left unscathed.

Across human skin, boils throb furiously.

If the emotional loss of shattered livelihoods wasn't torture enough, now every Egyptian cries out in physical agony. But from the sanctuary of his throne, Pharaoh himself remains unaffected. He still has no intention of surrender.

'Stop!' we shout. 'Enough!'
Our knees trembling, we look on in dismay.
This is annihilation.
This is torture.
How is this love?

'By now,' Yahweh tells the Egyptians, *'I could have used my power and caused a terrible disease that would have destroyed you and your people. I have let you live for this reason: to show you my power so that my name will be talked about in all the earth* (Ex. 9:15-16).'

Accused of callous cruelty, Yahweh has an alternative perspective: the punishments are restrained.

Accompanied by lightning, a thunderous hail storm erupts.

'Let the Israelites go to worship Yahweh *their God,'* Pharaoh's closest advisers beg. *'Don't you know that Egypt is ruined?* (Ex. 10:7)' But the king stands firm, refusing to relinquish his faith in Egypt's gods.

A plague of locusts strips all vegetation bare.

If it wasn't ruined before, now there really is no foreseeable recovery for Egypt's economy. Egypt's prosperity has been devoured to poverty, and at last the king is concerned. But letting the Israelites go, that would be foolish. The Israelite slaves now represent some of Egypt's only remaining wealth. Pharaoh is convinced: letting his slaves go would only make them stronger; they would become an even greater threat.

Three days of darkness engulfs the land.

Only now does Pharaoh concede his gods have lost. Even the mighty powers of Ra, controller of the sun, have been eclipsed. It is Yahweh instead who controls the elements. Indeed, the only Egyptian gods who remain undefeated are Pharaoh himself and the inheritor of his throne, Pharaoh's firstborn son.

'*I will punish all the gods of Egypt* (Ex. 12:12),' declares Yahweh. '*Every firstborn son in the land of Egypt will die* (Ex. 11:4-5).' No-one will be exempt, *from the firstborn of the king… to the firstborn of the prisoner in jail* (Ex. 12:29).

Fully deserved, this is Justice.

And Love demands it.

'*Tell the whole community of Israel,*' Yahweh continues, '*each man must get one lamb* (Ex. 12:3), *a one-year-old male that has nothing wrong with it* (Ex. 12:5). Get dressed ready for travel, kill the lamb, feast on it and celebrate. Tonight rescue is coming.

'*About midnight tonight I will go through all Egypt* (Ex. 11:4) and kill every firstborn son. But put some of the lamb's blood on your doorframes and w*hen I see the blood, I will pass over you* (Ex. 12:13).'

Entirely undeserved, this is Grace.

And Love provides it.

Hearing Egypt's excruciating cries of grief our knees give way as we crash to the ground. How is this love? How is this love? How is it fair that Yahweh *treats Israel differently from Egypt*? (Ex. 11:7) It's suffering for one and ecstasy for the other. Justice or Grace, how can both be of God? They seem so contradictory, so incompatible.

Tonight, as thousands lose their lives, Love sees the blood of an innocent lamb and judgement passes over the Israelites. But a day is coming when Love will see the blood of an innocent lamb and judgement will pass over all nationalities. On that day, Justice and Grace will hold hands, look each other in the eye, and kiss.

3.04 - From Death Comes Life

Cheers of euphoria are joined by the roar of pounding feet as the sight of a vast sea of bodies, hundreds of thousands, perhaps millions strong, floods Moses with immense pride. Gone are his hesitant nerves; this is the impossible dream, reality before his very eyes.

Just hours ago, Moses had seen Pharaoh's uncontrollable tears. 'Get out! *Leave my people,'* the king howled, bent over his son's cold, limp body, *'go and worship* Yahweh (Ex. 12:31).'

Though moved by such suffering, Moses had left the room unable to stifle a smile.

Because out from death, comes life for his people.

'Remember this day, the day you left Egypt (Ex. 13:3),' Moses shouts to the masses.

From now on every event must be viewed in the light of today.

This month will be the beginning of months (Ex. 12:2).

A new era has begun.

And by holding the mummified body of their great ancestor Joseph, Moses gets his message across in the most vivid way possible: the Israelites' future freedom builds upon past foundations. *'When God saves you,'* Joseph had declared in faith, *'remember to carry my bones with you out of Egypt* (Ex. 13:19).'

Moses is fulfilling Joseph's dying wish.

Still knelt by his son, the raucous sound of mass exodus, deafening like the crashing of waves, further ignites Pharaoh's rage. The king rises to his feet and watches from his palace window as wave after wave cross his nation's border and exit Egypt.

Soon this infatuation for Yahweh will be out of their systems, Pharaoh reassures himself. And once they return, he shall make them pay. These detestable Israelites have destroyed his nation. And they shall be the ones to rebuild it.

Then it dawns.

The crowds carry with them every possession they can.

These Israelites have no intention of return.

His eyes a furious blood-shot red, Pharaoh flings his fist into the wall.

'What have we done? We have lost our slaves! (Ex. 14:5)'

'Stop them!' he screeches, rushing from the room like a man possessed.

Yahweh leads the Israelites on their journey out of Egypt, guiding them by a remarkable pillar of cloud. Used to gods they can see and touch, the Father wants his children to come of age in no doubt of his presence with them, in no doubt that Yahweh saves.

The challenge of moving such substantial numbers, together with the scorching heat, makes progress slow. Reaching a large stretch of water, a rarity in the deserts beyond, Moses decides to make camp as evening draws in.

Exhausted, many take the opportunity to wash in the refreshing waters. Mothers watch their children closely, careful not to let them venture in too deep, beyond where reeds protrude the surface.

For a while laughter fills the air.

Before all of a sudden, the water starts to ripple, as if shaking angrily.

All turn to face the desert. Far off, a mighty sandstorm approaches. And the accompanying rumbling sound is ominously familiar. This is the storm of Egyptian horses and chariots charging at full pelt. The Israelites swing their heads back and forth, from desert to sea, as a terrifying realisation sets in.

There is no escape.

This is the end.

'What have you done to us, Moses? *Didn't we say to you in Egypt, "Leave us alone"?* (Ex. 14:11-12*) *Now we will die in the desert* (Ex. 14:12).'

'Don't be afraid!' Moses roars, bringing an unerring hush to the commotion. '*Stand still and you will see* Yahweh *save you today* (Ex. 14:13).'

Eyes open in amazement as Yahweh's pillar of cloud moves to directly intercept the course of the Egyptian galloping horses, and immediately the horses bolt, petrified by the dark, swirling fog. Drawing on all their years of experience, the Egyptian generals act quickly to bring the chaos under control. They halt their pursuit. The Israelites are trapped; there is no need to take unnecessary risks.

Next Moses - perfectly following orders - stretches his hand out over the waters.

Rushing eastward a gale blows in.

Colliding.

Driving.

Lashing back the waters.

Exposing the bed of reeds.

All night, faces etched with wonder and awe cross the partitioned seas, churning up the sodden surface. The Israelites reach land caked in dirt and overjoyed, now in no doubt: Yahweh saves.

On the other side of the water, shocked chariot drivers crack their whips, urging their horses forward in quick pursuit, charging onto the Israelite's wide walkway. Wheels toss mud high into the air, hooves sink into the quagmire; the chariots crash to a halt.

Total pandemonium ensues as reputable army generals fling themselves from their chariots. *'Let's get away from the Israelites!'* they shriek. *'Yahweh is fighting for them and against Egypt* (Ex. 14:25).'

As the sun rises on a brand new day, the storming winds cease.

Sending waves crashing down.

Some die on impact.

The rest flail in the depths until they can breathe no more.

From death comes life as Abraham's descendants dance in wild celebration. Watching on from the sanctuary of the floodplain, they spontaneously burst into song:

'Are there any gods like you, Yahweh?
There are no gods like you.
You are wonderful and holy,
Amazingly powerful,
A worker of miracles (Ex. 15:11).'

Encouraged and excited by new levels of understanding, trust and respect, the Community of Elohim reflect on their success. Today is a glimpse of their ultimate rescue intentions, where the whole of creation is brought out from slavery *into the glorious freedom of the children of God* (Rom. 8:21*).

'I'm so proud of Moses,' says one friend of Elohim whilst reaching down and energetically sketching a picture of fishing vessels caught in a torrential storm. In the image, one man stands unperturbed on the brow of his boat, winds and waves pelting his frame. Either the gale relents or all on the boat drown.

'*Quiet! Be still!* (Mark 4:39)' says the illustrator.

In the Artist's image the waters calm, cowering in retreat.

'*Who is this?*' one friend asks with a knowing, playful grin, pointing at the man in the picture. '*Even the winds and waves obey him!* (Mark 4:41)'

Laughing, two friends lovingly wrap arms around the third.

'*This is my Son, whom I love; with him I am well pleased* (Matt. 3:17*).'

3.05 - The Proposal

Across a solid blue backdrop rich golden rays fill the sky. Energetic beams bounce off the sands causing a dazzling sparkle all around. Exposed to the sun, the desert floor burns scorching hot.

And on sore, blistered, throbbing feet, hundreds of thousands of Israelites trudge.

Trudge.

Trudge.

Trudge.

Every man, woman and child drips with sweat, desperate for shade. All joy has gone. Hot and hostile conditions may have been common as slaves, but nothing compared to this.

'What kind of freedom is this?' the first mutters arise.

'It is more like torture.'

'*Is* Yahweh *with us or not? (Ex. 17:7)*'

'Soon we will starve to death.'

'At least in Egypt we could eat *cucumbers, melons, leeks, onions and garlic* (Num. 11:5).'

'*It would have been better if* Yahweh *had killed us in the land of Egypt* (Ex. 16:3).'

We jolt. From our experience so far, we can sense God's heartbreak. After everything they've just been through, how... how can they be so insulting? After everything, how can they possibly question whether Yahweh is for them?

Bemused, we step back. Maybe the Israelite's reaction is understandable. Yahweh is after all proposing a monumental shift in mind-set. To them, Yahweh is just one of many gods. The concept of only one all-powerful, all-encompassing God, well, they just cannot wrap their minds round it.

The Israelites stand in sheer amazement as bread *like small white seeds* (Ex. 16:31) falls from the sky. The never-before-seen food is delicious, tasting *like wafers made from honey* (Ex. 16:31). Every day the camp is covered in a fresh, abundant layer.

As well as providing physically, Yahweh also emphasises to his fledgling society the importance of their emotional well-being. Every seventh day will be a *day of rest* (Ex. 16:25), a day to celebrate their freedom, a day to remember that the constant non-stop labour of slavery is no more.

To help distinguish the day, no food will fall on a day of rest. Instead, on the sixth day of each week Yahweh will provide *enough food for two days* (Ex. 16:30). God's instruction is simple: do not search for food on a day of rest. Instead, collect twice as much the day before.

The sun rises on the first day of rest.

And several Israelites set out in search of food.

'*How long will you people refuse to obey my commands and teachings? (Ex. 16:28)*' Yahweh sighs. The cry is filled with poignancy. The failure to follow such a simple instruction is deeply concerning; soon the Rescue Strategists want to unveil hundreds of new instructions for living.

In a highly significant new covenant.

Promises given to Noah and Abraham continue to shape the Rescue Mission's future. And in this respect, the third covenant will be no different. But in other ways it will differ. Until now Yahweh's covenants have, in the most part, been unconditional. They have been incessant and generous one-way displays of affections, regardless of response.

But Love desires response.

Partnership.

Collaboration.

Commitment.

This time the contract will be proposed before it is signed.

The Rescuer knows that this is a society in desperate need of some structure; and significance. Second class citizens their entire lives, those brought out from slavery will be invited to play their part in the liberation of the entire world. If chosen, the new nation of Israel will stand out. If chosen, Elohim's manifesto for living will advertise the Creator's character. If chosen, all nations will be attracted towards an alternative, healthier lifestyle. If chosen, creation will take a giant leap towards the paradise originally intended for it.

No more murder.

No more adultery.

No more robbery.

No more deception.

No more jealousy.

But having spent their entire lives embedded in Egyptian culture, with no cultural identity of their own, can the Israelites truly change their ways? With so much at stake, can they do it for their Rescuer? Can they do it for their Lover?

On the day his life transformed from obscurity to significance, Moses stood by the Mount of Sinai and heard a voice from flickering flames promise, *'This will be the proof that I am sending you: after you lead the people out of Egypt, all of you will worship me on this mountain* (Ex. 3:12).'

And *exactly three months after* leaving *Egypt* (Ex. 19:1), the Israelites reach the Desert of Sinai. At the foot of the mountain they make camp.

Moses smiles wide, satisfied and besotted, revelling in the proof that it is Yahweh, and Yahweh alone who has brought the Israelites out of Egypt.

Yahweh is smiling too. After months of wooing the ones he loves so dearly, their devotion excites.

'Every one of you,' the proposal begins, *'has seen what I did to the people of Egypt. You saw how I carried you out of Egypt as if on eagle's wings... (Ex. 19:4)'*

I choose you.

I love you.

'...And I brought you here to me (Ex. 19:4).'

I want relationship.

The Lover gets down on one knee.

'If you obey me and keep my agreement, you will be my own possession, chosen from all nations (Ex. 19:5). *You must not use gold or silver to make idols for yourself* (Ex. 20:23). *You must not have any other gods except me* (Ex. 20:3).'

55

Will you choose me?
Will you love me?
Will you marry me?

Apprehension rises in our gut. Repeated rejection has scarred the Rescue Mission so far. And so soon after epic, indisputable liberation, the Israelites have already dismissed it as meaningless. Their affections appear far from consistent and yet God is proposing a relationship of permanent, exclusive, mutual love. This is a risk.

Thick, dramatic cloud covers the mountain.
Thunder and lightning roars.
Everyone trembles.
And the Lover's heart skips a beat, awaiting response.

Yes. Yes, we choose you.
'*We will do everything that* Yahweh *has said* (Ex. 24:7).'
Yes, we love you.
The answer is unanimous.
Yes, we will marry you.

With a spring in their step, Moses and seventy-three Israelite leaders make their way up the mountain and in a remarkable celebration of intimacy they meet the God of Israel. They see his feet on a spectacular surface, *like a pavement made of sapphire, clear as the sky itself* (Ex. 24:10).

Below the mountain a statue made of gold takes form.
'*Israel,*' it is announced, '*these are your gods who brought you out of the land of Egypt* (Ex. 32:4).'

3.06 - What Deserves Punishment

Equipped with an overwhelming 'yes' to God's marriage proposal, Moses climbs alone, higher into the remote, rocky mountain tops. In Elohim's presence every moment is alight with frenetic creative energy.

'*I will live with the people of Israel and be their God (Ex. 29:45),*' Yahweh announces, each syllable loaded with absolute delight. Love's heart is leaping triumphantly; relationship on earth with humans, this has always been Love's ultimate desire.

Below the mountain, a statue made of gold takes form.

Moses has been up the mountain, flashing with furious fire, for over a month now. By now he must surely have met his end, either choked in a cloud of smoke, or burnt in a ball of flames. The fledgling society can wait no longer. They need a new leader, and fast.

So they sculpt a calf similar in appearance to the Egyptian god Hathor.

'*Israel,*' it is announced, '*these are your gods who brought you out of the land of Egypt (Ex. 32:4).*'

In complete shock, Yahweh freezes.

Silence ensues.

Though he doesn't know why, Moses feels a numb pain, a great emptiness draw over him.

Eventually, a hurt quivering voice breaks the hush. '*Your people,*' the voice tells Moses, '*whom you brought out of Egypt, have become corrupt. They have quickly turned away from what I commanded them (Ex. 32:7).*'

Drenched in sadness, the words break Moses' heart. Now it is stressed that he, not Yahweh, rescued the Israelites from Egypt.

Absorbing the revelation, Moses begins to fume. Every muscle tightens. He breathes heavily, in and out through the nose; then bows his head, and shuts his eyes. Struck by another lengthy silence, it dawns on Moses that his anger must pale in comparison to God's own heartbroken fury. Moses is ashamed. And scared.

'Now leave me alone (Ex. 32:10*),' Yahweh's voice still heavy and torn tells Moses. *'I am so angry... that I am going to destroy* these people. *Then I will make you and your descendants a great nation (Ex. 32:10).'*

Our stomach clenches. We begin to tremble in fear. Our cheeks burn red and sweat drips from our forehead down into our eyes.

God is petrifying.

Frightening.

Terrifying.

For the first time in this room, we feel lost in a lonely, silent void. We sit crumpled in a heap, still and numb, regretting our compulsion to enter this Headquarters. Ignorance was bliss. What's more, if God has indeed been in this room, as all evidence clearly indicates, then he may come back sometime soon. And we do not want to be here when he does.

But if we leave now, unanswered questions could eat away at us for years to come.

Like how, how, how could God, how could Love, destroy those who are chosen, set apart, those desired as a treasured possession?

Horrifying images of the Phase One flood submerge our mind, violently smashing 'I am going to destroy' into frenzied shards, like the debris of a shipwreck. Likewise, the plan to make Moses' descendants a great nation, crashes ferociously against the rocks. Echoing the Phase Two promises, a fresh start would wipe out so much progress since Abraham. Does the Rescue Strategist really want that? A blank slate, a new society, may be easier to educate in the progressive, healthy ways of Yahweh but doesn't this generation deserve a chance to change? They may be so set in their ways, so entrenched in Egyptian culture, but come on, is that really a reason to destroy?!

But our distress, we decide, will make no difference.

God says, 'Leave me alone.'

Braced for the onset of suffering, reluctantly we pick our slumped frame from up off the floor. A tear slides: destruction is coming. God doesn't change his mind.

Tears streaming down his cheeks, Moses falls to his knees. He shakes his arms, as if beating his chest, and begs, *'Yahweh, don't let your anger destroy your people, whom you brought out of Egypt (Ex. 32:11).*

Remember the men who served you - Abraham, Isaac and Israel (Ex. 32:13). Remember your promises.'

Another tense, prolonged silence ensues.

Before Yahweh changes *his mind* (Ex. 32:14).

In the midst of our surprise and relief, a banner at the top of a large blue poster catches our eye. *'I am offering you life or death, blessings or curses,'* the banner reads. *'Now, choose life! (Deut. 30:19)'*

Absorbed, we brush away a tear.

Creatively filled with scraps of paper, this poster outlines the consequences of keeping or breaking God's manifesto for living, the new laws of Israel. On the left, 'Peace,' 'Protection,' 'Victory,' stand out, vibrantly coloured. Interwoven within, gorgeous golden italics add, *'I will place my Holy Tent among you. I will walk with you (Lev. 26:11-12).'*

Recognising God's dream of intimacy, we smile and whisper, 'Choose life.'

In contrast, the right-hand side of the collage turns dark. Tangled together like a constrictive web, a mesh of words includes, 'Destruction,' 'Disease' and 'Starvation.' Death: this is the consequence of disobedience, the result of choosing self-depredation.

'Choose life,' we urge again, this time with a lump in our throat.

Then, in the centre of the poster, in elegant, vivid white, we read, *'If these disobedient people are sorry for what they did and accept punishment for their sin, I will remember my agreement* (Lev. 26:41-42). I will not *completely destroy them* (Lev. 26:45).'

Sin: the word catches our attention. It appears to encapsulate every kind of disobedience, every boundary broken.

Sin, we conjecture, is what corrupts beauty.

Sin is what causes division.

Sin is what deserves punishment.

Yet remorse over sin, God has revealed, will ensure the Rescue Mission's continuation.

Below the mountain Israelites sing and dance in honour of a recently constructed golden calf.

Livid and distraught, and soaked by his tears, Moses bows low before Yahweh. Fuelled by compassion and remorse, slowly but surely an offer leaves his lips.

'Please forgive them this sin,' Moses pleads. *'If you will not, then erase my name from the book in which you have written the names of your people* (Ex. 32:32).'

Though wracked with grief, the Community of Elohim somehow manages a smile. Though his offer will not be accepted, Moses' selfless proposal has connected with the heart of Love's Rescue Mission.

In place of those that deserve punishment, one innocent man will offer himself.

3.07 - You Shall Save Three Thousand

Dead bodies lie scattered across blood soaked ground. A chilling silence fills the air; a silence completely contrasting recent celebrations of a golden calf, a silence pierced only by sporadic grief stricken howls.

Moses' face is stained with sorrow. Tears have left lines tracing down through his dirt and dust smeared cheeks. The leader feels sick; not just because of the horrific sight or the ghastly stench, but because he, Moses, had to instigate these deaths. He gave the order for this purge of three-thousand Israelites.

How did it come to this, Moses wonders? How did a celebration of exclusive covenant with their Liberator turn so quickly into three thousand funerals? What more could he have done? He'd smashed the stone tablets containing the law - didn't that demonstrate the severity of their crime? He'd even offered everyone an opportunity for forgiveness, declaring, '*Let anyone who wants to follow* Yahweh *come to me* (Ex. 32:26).'

But only the family of Levi stepped forward to choose Yahweh.

They chose life.

The rest stood firm, stubborn in their rejection, seeing nothing wrong in their construction of other gods to worship and honour.

They chose death.

'But, but, but...'

Whether God is listening or not we want to shout out in protest.

But we do not dare. Fear holds our mouth shut.

We want to tell God that in many ways we understand. We get that Love requires justice. We get that broken laws must carry consequences. And we get that punishments will deter future anarchy. We get all that. But isn't this meant to be a Rescue Mission? At the moment this is just slaughter.

God, we would urge, if we dared, you need to find some other way to deal with sin.

Full of compassionate sorrow, Moses looks around at those shaking in grief and in their haunted, petrified eyes he sees a deep, tortured regret: at last all have grasped the significance of keeping the law. God was not exaggerating: death really is the consequence of disobedience.

So too is separation.

Moses cannot bring himself to share this horrifying revelation with the mourners; not yet anyway - it still aches in his heart too much. Their relationship with Yahweh is over. The Israelites will have to journey on toward the Promised Land without the company and guidance of their Protector. God has withdrawn his presence, because in his own words, '*I might destroy you on the way* (Ex. 33:3).'

Moses shudders.

The future is hopeless.

His Israelites are a trembling rabble of ex-slaves.

And the Promised Land is home to fierce, experienced warriors.

On their own, the Israelites don't stand a chance.

To attack would be suicide.

Once again, we are left stunned. We cannot believe what we are reading. How does God ever expect to fulfil his dream of intimacy with humans, if his very presence kills them?

God, we would urge again, if we dared shout out, you need to find some other way to deal with sin.

United in grief, mourning the loss of three thousand dearly-loved lives, three friends find comfort in each other's tender affection. The Community of Elohim grip each other tightly, desperate to contain all their devastated anger within their embrace.

The community may have had to withdraw from relationship, but pure, pulsating, mesmerised Love is unable to avert its gaze. The trio are watching on, intrigued and enthralled, as Moses sets about constructing an elegant tent from *fine linen and blue, purple and red thread* (Ex. 26:1). Before the golden calf heartbreak, this was the tent that Yahweh had instructed Moses to build; the tent which would house Yahweh's presence during their journey to the Promised Land.

Hope rises in the embracing Elohim.

'Look how much Moses wants us,' shouts the Father, a smile returning to his face. 'Moses still believes relationship is possible.'

'With faith like this, Abba, rescue and relationship are still possible. Now is the time...' the Son pauses in suspense, overtaken by excitement. 'Now is the time to unveil our plan to deal with sin.'

'Yes, Son, the blood of an animal shall be spilt instead of the blood of a guilty human. This sacrifice is justice and grace holding hands, giving our children a chance to start again in pursuit of beauty.'

'Then we will be able to live together with humans,' adds the third friend in Elohim, 'engaged for marriage.'

'Oh, Ruach, my love, you shall live in the glorious room that Moses will place in his tent. They shall call it the 'Holy of Holies,' because you are so stunningly beautiful.'

'I cannot wait,' says Ruach, her eyes shining with delight. 'Then only the thickness of a curtain will separate us from humans.'

'We shall allow one man once a year, washed clean and wearing *holy clothes* (Lev. 16:4), to step beyond the curtain into the Holy of Holies. It shall be a glorious moment.'

'He will be a priest from the tribe of Levi; reward for choosing our love when others did not.'

'And once a year this priest shall confess over a living goat *all the sins and crimes of Israel... Then he will send the goat away into the desert* (Lev. 16:21).'

'Yes! That way our loved ones will physically see their sins running away from them, never to return again. The sight should convince them that their sins really are no more; that they really are forgiven, free and clean.'

'Let's also replace the stone slabs which Moses smashed, and put them in the Holy of Holies in a majestic wooden chest.'

'And let's establish an annual festival to ensure no-one ever forgets these events at Sinai. *On the day of firstfruits* (Num. 28:26), celebrating a bountiful harvest, our children shall reflect upon the beginnings of our relationship, and remember the tragic loss of three thousand.'

'Taking place fifty days after Passover, the event shall become known as Pentecost. And at one future Pentecost, after the world-changing events of that year's Passover, Ruach, you shall save three-thousand lives (Acts 2:41).'

'I shall put the law *in their minds, and write it on their hearts* (Jer. 31:33*).'

Laughing with joy, Abba gives Ruach an appreciative kiss. 'You are so beautiful, my love. Come, let's go. Let's speak to Moses *face to face as a man speaks with a friend* (Ex. 33:11).'

'Oh, how his face shall shine,' Rauch replies, grinning wildly. 'Come, let's fill Moses' marvellous tent.'

Ruach takes hold of Abba's hand.

'Let's go travelling with our fiancé.'

3.08 - The Splattered Mess

Joshua may not be able to sleep but it's not because of the blazing fire high above the tabernacle; by now he has grown accustomed to Yahweh's flames lighting up the night. Instead, he is just too excited. Joshua is like a child on the eve of a great celebration. Frenetic thoughts are racing without restraint, and they will continue to do so until Moses' now familiar trumpet call greets the dawn; the dawning of the day that Joshua has been waiting for his entire life, the day that the Israelites reach the Promised Land.

Head resting on his elbow, Joshua lies with eyes affectionately fixed upon Yahweh's ferocious flames. Not since the fledgling days of his youth, has love felt like this. Where once mysterious, far-off powers could only be revered in the form of lifeless carvings, rigid and static, this god Yahweh draws close, swirling and flickering with wild animation. Fire by night, cloud by day this god who steals the heart watches and protects with unprecedented intimacy.

For the last eleven days Yahweh has led the way north from Sinai with authority, patience and provision. Where Yahweh moved, the Israelites followed. Traversing hot and hostile deserts, their route even took in a long refreshing coastline, rich in nutritious quail.

Now the Israelites camp on the brink of a lush and fertile land.

Not that Joshua has ever seen the land, of course; no-one has. To the Israelites the entire world is simply an endless vista of golden sands, the occasional oasis of water and clumps of jagged mountains. The only paradise they've ever glimpsed was in the north-east of Egypt, a sumptuous land of flowing rivers and thriving greenery. But even that was a relatively small region. Can an entire land really be filled with green?

But Joshua sees no reason to doubt Yahweh's promise now. Even though this was a land cursed long ago by Noah, even though it was gripped by crippling drought the last time Canaan was home to Abraham's descendants, Joshua's conviction is unwavering: if this God can liberate slaves, then this God can transform a desolate curse into a prosperous blessing.

Joshua can sense it in his guts.

Today is the day.

The day the Israelites reach the Promised Land.

Joshua knows that victory is possible. If slavery had any benefits then at least it made the Israelites strong and disciplined. Even before they reached Sinai, Joshua led an Israelite army to victory over the Amalekites. And now, over a year later, they are ready for greater battles. They are trained, drilled, and tactically united. For the last eleven days all tribes have marched in a strict regimented formation encircling Yahweh's elegant tabernacle.

Lost in love, Joshua grins. *'You keep your loving promise,'* his heart sings, *'and lead the people you have saved (Ex. 15:2).'* Over and over Moses' liberation lyrics play silently in his mind, passing the hours until bright shining light emerges from the east to welcome the day.

The day the Israelites conquer the Promised Land.

Under a rich blue sky, Joshua climbs to the peak of Canaan's mountainous border. Standing with arms outstretched, wind blowing through his hair, Joshua feels light enough to fly; indeed his heart is soaring. He is looking out at a panorama of paradise, an unending ocean of greenery.

'You keep your loving promise and lead the people you have saved.' This time there is no holding back Joshua's volume. *'With your strength you will guide them to your holy place (Ex. 15:13).'*

Caleb too feels on top of the world. Wrapping his arm over Joshua's shoulders he adds, *'We should certainly go up and take the land for ourselves. We can certainly do it (Num. 13: 30).'*

Joshua nods: soon this heaven on earth will be theirs.

Soon.

Not today, like he had predicted last night.

But soon.

Tactically, Moses was right to survey enemy territory before attacking. The Israelites cannot afford any mistakes.

This is a once in a life-time opportunity.

Any offensive should not be rushed.

Paradise is worth waiting for.

Night has fallen and in the light of Yahweh's flames, the Israelite camp is in chaos. Not a sole is asleep; all are engaged in a ferocious war of words as rumours and misconstrued truths spread and multiply like a disease, unleashing a cowering fear, contaminating, choking, crushing, destroying all hope.

'*We can't attack these people; they are stronger than we are* (Num. 13:31).'

'They are ruthless warriors.'

'Champions of combat.'

'Bloodthirsty giants.'

'With modern weapons.'

'And monstrous city walls.'

'*We wish we had died in Egypt or in this desert* (Num. 14:2).'

'*Let's choose a leader and go back to Egypt* (Num. 14:4).'

Outcast from the mayhem, Joshua and Caleb sit with legs clutched tight to their chests, weighed down by great grief. Half-naked, having torn their clothes, the pair tremble as if the ground is shaking beneath them.

'*Don't turn against* Yahweh!' the pair had begged until their throats throbbed. '*Don't be afraid of the people in that land! We will chew them up. They have no protection but* Yahweh *is with us* (Num. 14:7-9).'

But they may as well have been shouting to an empty desert.

And now the verdict, the final judgement of Yahweh has been delivered. For the next forty years the fire and smoke presence of Yahweh will be staying put. As requested by the masses there will be no advance on Canaan. This entire generation of Israelites - all except young Joshua and Caleb - have squandered their chance of paradise.

Slumped beside a pile of rotting fruit, meaningless mementos from a rejected better world, Joshua picks up a pomegranate and in an eruption of fury hurls the fruit far into the desert. The explosion, the splattered mess, the waste of such precious juice - for Joshua this sums it all up.

His generation has thrown away the chance of eating such succulent fruit every day. They have flung paradise through the air. And have themselves come crashing down in the desert.

Postponed for forty years, the great homecoming has been cancelled. The wait for heaven on earth goes on.

3.09 - He Meets a Man

East of the Jordan River (Deut. 1:5) an elderly man steps forward onto an elevated rocky plateau and an almighty army falls perfectly silent. Overwhelmed with respect, no-one wants to miss a word from their one hundred and twenty year old leader.

Moses clears his throat.

For forty years he has been preparing for this moment; his farewell speech, the speech that will shape his legacy. If he is nervous, it doesn't show. His voice reverberates off the mountains and across the open expanse.

'Yahweh *your God has made you grow... There are as many of you as there are stars in the sky* (Deut. 1:10).'

By referencing one of the Rescue Mission's foundational promises, Moses makes a stirring start. This army, this entirely new generation of Israelites must know that they are living in the fulfilment of Abraham's great faith. To take hold of the freedom their parents let slip, they too must have great faith.

'Yahweh *your God has protected you while you travelled through this great desert.* For forty years *you have had everything you needed* (Deut. 2:7).'

An additional note on the Phase Three wall informs us that the Israelite population only shrunk slightly over their four decades in the desert. What's more, neither their *clothes nor sandals wore out* (Deut. 29:5).

Living in such harsh conditions, this is incredible. This is clear testament to the continuing care of Yahweh. Throughout a long and enduring punishment, God clearly did not abandon his children.

To the left of the text we find a sketch of a map outlining the Israelites' recent travels. Instead of heading north and entering Canaan by its mountainous south, they journeyed east through Edom then north into Moab. It's not the route that we would have taken - it's longer and leaves the Israelites still needing to cross a sizeable river - but we are not too concerned. The Rescuer must have his motives for the move.

What is really holding our attention is a comment on the map about Edom: Moses says that God gave this land to the descendants of Esau (Deut. 2:4). We turn ninety degrees left, back to the wall of Phase Two, to refresh our memory. Esau was the brother who sold his inheritance rights to his younger sibling Jacob, now known as Israel.

And in doing so, he threw away his rights to the land of Canaan.

But the nation of Esau still exists. God gave Esau's descendants the land of Edom, south east of Canaan.

Which intrigues us: God's actions seem to be stretching far beyond the text displayed in this Headquarters. Like tributaries of a mighty river, the Rescue Mission has undocumented subplots.

'You are the children of Yahweh (Deut. 14:1),' Moses' speech continues. *'He has chosen you from all the people on earth to be his very own* (Deut. 14:2). *Know in your heart that* Yahweh *corrects you as a parent corrects a child (Deut. 8:5).'*

Moses' words spark a sensation within us that we haven't felt for quite a while: a sense of pleasure.

Recently we have been struck by a sickness in our stomach, shaken by the punishments that made Yahweh more akin to a tyrannous dictator than a compassionate lover.

But Moses' perspective stills our stomach.

To him, these were the actions of a parent correcting a child.

'Love Yahweh *your God with all your heart, all your soul and all your strength* (Deut. 6:5). Yahweh *did not care for you and choose you because there are many of you - you are the smallest nation of all. But* Yahweh *chose you because he loved you, and he kept his promise to your ancestors* (Deut. 7:7).

'Pay careful attention to the words I have said,' concludes Moses, the volume of his voice reaching a final crescendo. *'These should not be unimportant words for you, but rather they mean life to you!* (Deut. 32:46-47)'

'Choose life,' Abba pleads passionately.

'Choose life like Moses.'

'After all those days spent basking in our presence, Moses has become a glorious example of humanity's great potential.'

Ruach dances with rapid animation. 'My breath has brought him life. But *my Spirit shall not remain in human beings forever… they will live only one hundred and twenty years* (Gen. 6:3).'

'You are right,' smiles Abba, recognising the significance of Ruach's words. The words were once stained in the most searing of pains. Today they are painted with pride.

'*Though his eyes* are *not weak and he* is *still strong* (Deut. 34:7), it is time for Moses to join us. His leadership shall pass on to Joshua. Joshua shall lead his army across the Jordan River and into battle.'

'Joshua. That's a great name. It means "Yahweh saves."'

Father and Son look into each other's shimmering eyes; reflected back they see the love they both feel. 'Joshua is also the name of my beloved Son,' Abba grins, 'Joshua means the same as Jesus.'

'Father, at Sinai our children asked not to look at *"this terrible fire anymore* (Deut. 18:16)." *What they have said is good* (Deut. 18:17). Our flames may show we are alive and animated but they are hardly relational.'

'Soon, Jesus, we will have a presence on earth that the Israelites can eat and laugh and have conversations with.'

'Oh, Abba, every day I look forward to that moment.'

Having climbed *Mount Nebo from the plains of Moab* (Deut. 34:1), a one hundred and twenty year old man steps out onto a rocky plateau and looks out across the Jordan River to a gloriously green fertile land, the land *promised to Abraham, Isaac and Jacob* (Deut. 34:4). After forty years in the desert, Moses can smell it; they are so close now, so close to his life's great ambition, so close to paradise.

Moses falls to his knees and lays his head down on the rocks.

And with his eyes fixed firmly on paradise, *Moses, the servant of Yahweh,* dies (Deut. 34:5).

Fifteen hundred years later, dressed *in heavenly glory* (Luke 9:31), Moses finally enters the Promised Land.

And in the nation of Israel, he meets a man named Jesus.

3.10 - Completing Phase Three

Swords slice limbs.

Smoke chokes lungs.

Flames char flesh.

The limbs, lungs and flesh of innocent screaming children.

Trembling with grief, sick to the stomach, three friends screw their eyes shut tight. Locked in intimate, loving embrace, tears stream from the eyes of Jesus, Ruach and Abba. The sights and sounds of these sacrificed children, these so-called acts of 'worship' to please and appease Canaanite gods, rip at Elohim's heart.

To an outsider, like an Israelite, Canaan might seem civilised and advanced. The nation has prospered in the textile and timber industries and boasts sophisticated fortified cities with water supplies and drainage. An outsider might be tempted to think that Canaan's gods deserve respect for such success. In fact, the Israelites might even be tempted to think that Canaan's gods aren't that dissimilar from theirs.

After all, Canaan's father of all gods is called El.

And Canaan's most active god is named Baal, meaning 'Lord.'

But scratch a bit deeper, like the Community of Elohim do and tears begin to fall. These gods, these constructions of the human imagination, couldn't be more different from Elohim's loving embrace. Trust in these gods has led to a culture containing child sacrifice, savage barbaric violence and rampant, demeaning sex.

Even sex with relatives and animals (Lev. 18:23-24).

Having grown up exclusively in the desert, Abba has kept his children unexposed to these practices. Yet already, whilst heading towards Canaan, some have been unable to resist the temptation *to worship Baal* (Num. 25:3). Yahweh's covenant partner, Yahweh's shining light to the nations, has already stepped onto a slope which descends to debilitating darkness.

The tragedy brought Moses to tears during his farewell speech: *'When you cross the Jordan River and enter the land Yahweh is giving you, don't learn to do the hateful things the other nations do.'* No onlooker could ever forget the unerring urgency in his voice. *'Don't let anyone among you offer a son or daughter as a sacrifice in the fire...* Yahweh *hates anyone who does these things. Because the other nations do these things* Yahweh *will force them out of the land ahead of you* (Deut. 18:9-13).'

For centuries Love has been holding back punishment on Canaan (Gen. 15:16), patiently longing and hoping for some chink of light, some glimmer of original beauty that would cause Canaan's numerous nationalities to realise the horror of their actions.

The light never emerged.

Now all hope has faded to black.

Love has been left with no other option.

The embracing Elohim roars out in excruciating agony.

The earth shudders and shakes with ferocious rage.

Flinging fast-flowing waves high into the air.

Exposing the wide-reaching Jordan riverbed.

And in a scene which echoes their parent's momentous escape from Egypt, the *people of Israel* walk *across on dry land* (Josh. 3:17). Overwhelmed with amazement they enter the land promised to their ancestor Abraham, revelling in the evidence of Yahweh's unfathomable affection.

Now it is time to fight.

All who are willing and able (Deut. 20:8) stand confident and ready, *dressed for war* (Josh. 4:12).

'*When you march up to attack a city, first make them an offer of peace,*' Joshua instructs. '*But if they do not make peace with you...* Yahweh *will give* the city *to you* (Deut. 20:10-13).'

The Israelites surround the perimeter walls of Jericho, a monumental city on top of a hill.

For seven days they wait.

No acceptance of peace, no semblance of repentance arises.

The earth quakes as another excruciating cry grieves the great darkness.

Jericho's walls come crashing down.

'*Completely destroy these people,*' Joshua roars as pandemonium ensues. '*Otherwise, they will teach you what they do for their gods* (Deut. 20:16-18).'

Swords slice limbs.

Smoke chokes lungs.

Flames char flesh.

Mourning their loss, feeling the full agony of the bloodshed, Jesus, Ruach and Abba grip each other tight. To have to resort to such destruction hurts Love to the core. But, looking into each other's eyes, seeing the tears stream, the trio know that this pain today is necessary; eradicating the spine-chilling practice of child sacrifice, this is another step towards restoring creation to its originally intended paradise.

Heading west then south, Joshua leads his army on an intelligent sweeping offensive. The Israelites discover a land in economic and political turmoil - a direct consequence of Egypt's humiliation four decades ago - and at times their conquests are straightforward.

Canaan's fortified cities however, present a much tougher challenge. To conquer the city of Ai, near to Bethel, Joshua implements a shrewd and incisive ambush, luring the enemy out from behind their walls and exposing their fortress to the infiltration of secretly stationed Israelites.

Having lived in Ai and Bethel themselves, the slick and sophisticated success would have made Abraham and Jacob proud. What's more, if Moses was here now, he'd be delighted to see his people discarding their portable tents to dwell in more permanent structures.

Abba's children begin life in paradise: a *land with rivers and pools of water, with springs that flow in the valleys and hills, a land that has wheat and barley, vines, fig trees, pomegranates, olive oil and honey;* a land where, as Moses put it, '*you will have everything you need* (Deut. 8:7-9).'

Phase Three is complete.

Now the Rescuer's thoughts can turn to even greater ambitions.

During the absolute anarchy of Jericho's demise, Rahab, a Canaanite prostitute - a symbol of Jericho's detested promiscuous culture - was rescued. Pulled out from the engulfing flames, her surprising redemption symbolises the task appointed to Israel in Phase Four.

'*As slaves in Egypt you were ashamed,*' Yahweh announces, '*but I have removed that shame* (Josh. 5:9).' News of Israel's achievements will spread like aftershocks across the globe, catching the attention of significant rulers. Now Israel possesses respect.

'Who is this powerful Yahweh?' they will ask.

Israel has been blessed to be a blessing.

They have been rescued to bring rescue.

Loved to be love.

They must tell the world of Yahweh's great marriage proposal.

They must share their invitation to be the Bride in God's glorious wedding.

Because when the whole earth is united in intimacy with its Lover, there will be no more pain.

No more war, discrimination or destruction.

Every tear will have been wiped away.

PHASE FOUR

4.01 - Violence is Spiralling

Self-consciousness is a powerful thing. Though we have been alone for several hours, and even though inwardly we are riddled with doubt, outwardly we are straining to portray a smile.

The text on the Phase Three wall concluded with the Israelites declaring, '*We will never stop following* Yahweh *to serve other gods!* (Josh. 24:16)' And for all we know, Yahweh probably started dancing when he heard the words.

But for us, the declaration only fills us with scepticism.

It's just that we have heard it all before.

Each time the promise is quickly broken.

Maybe we could believe it this time if Canaan didn't still remain a cosmopolitan hotbed of competing cultures; if the Rescuer's ambition for a completely new and fresh society, free from the shackles of the old ways, had actually been realised.

But it hasn't. A map on the Phase Three wall shows us that at the time of Joshua's death, interwoven among Israel's twelve tribes there are Sidonians, Mesopotamians, Amorites, Canaanites, Perizzites, Hivites, Jebusites, Ammonites, Hittites, Moabites, Edomites, Amalekites and Philistines.

Perhaps the Israelites have here the ideal opportunity to progress Yahweh's Phase Four aspirations. Surrounded by so many nationalities they have an opportunity to share Yahweh's progressive desires for society.

A society with justice at its core.

A society where violence never spirals out of control.

A society where revenge is restricted by the principle of *life for life, eye for eye, tooth for tooth, hand for hand, foot for foot, burn for burn, wound for wound and bruise for bruise* (Ex. 21:24-25).

But what if Yahweh's covenant partner fails to stand out from the crowd? What if Abba's Bride becomes attracted to the contrasting and constricting ways of Baal? What if she becomes like her neighbours, lashing out spontaneously, ignoring 'eye for an eye'? Won't they drag Yahweh down with them? United in relationship aren't the two inextricably linked? Won't the actions of one directly affect the reputation of the other?

By aligning himself with the Israelites, Yahweh's name could become a laughing-stock; it could become a by-word for humiliation.

For failure.

Sweat slides from our armpits.

When the stakes are so high, and when he is equipped with such miraculous power, it horrifies us to think that God could have taken such a risk.

But this is Love.

And Love trusts.

Love hands over its heart.

Love draws alongside.

Love sees potential.

Because Love desires, Love requires, relationship.

The realisation refreshes us like rippling rain and as a smile, now undoubtedly genuine, returns to our face, we turn to our right to face the wall of Phase Four.

To our surprise, apart from a few posters attached to the right-hand side, the wall is mostly empty. Even a sturdy wooden desk in front of the wall, with chair tucked beneath, has nothing on it. All we can find is a small metallic torch in one of the desk's drawers. We swiftly pocket the torch; it could come in handy. After all, the limp light fitting which dangles from the ceiling of this old room holds no bulb.

Then we see it.

Directly above our head: a hatch.

A square doorway in the ceiling with, 'Phase Four – Enter if you dare,' etched upon it.

It's almost as if we don't read the final four words as adrenaline takes hold and our tiring muscles experience resurgence. In a flash we have lifted the chair on top of the desk, clambered up, pushed open the hatch and pulled our re-energised frame up through the opening.

The disconcerting darkness, the puffs of rising dust, the cobwebs clinging mercilessly, the damp clamminess, and a reek worse than the stench of our armpits, all stun simultaneously, causing us to cough and splutter and fall over in a heap.

Slumped in the darkness, apprehensive and alone, only now do we truly pay regard to the warning scratched onto the hatch. By clambering up here unreservedly, only now do we begin to wonder whether we might have in fact made a terrible mistake.

Then we remember the torch: though it only sends forth a narrow beam, its light is enough to reveal a loft filled with hanging narratives and diagrams. Not knowing where to begin, we brush away the cobwebs and flash the torch onto pages closest to us:

'The *children grew up and did not know* Yahweh *or what he had done for Israel. So they did what* Yahweh *said was wrong, and they worshipped the Baal idols* (Jud. 2:10).

Our every muscle clenches.
We flick the torch elsewhere:

A physically strong and socially privileged Israelite, Samson can take one look at a Philistine woman and shout, '*Get that woman for me! She is the one I want!* (Jud. 14:3)'
Within days Samson has married the Philistine.
Yet at his wedding feast, the Philistines humiliate Samson.
So Samson storms out and kills thirty Philistines.
In retaliation, Samson's wife is *given to his best man* (Jud. 14:20).
So Samson ties torches to the tails of three hundred foxes and lets them *loose in the grain fields of the Philistines* (Jud. 15:5).
In retaliation, *the Philistines* burn *Samson's wife and her father to death* (Jud. 15:6).
So Samson pounds and pummels and crushes one thousand Philistines using only a donkey's jawbone.

We shudder.
Cultures are merging.
An 'eye for an eye' is being ignored.
Violence is spiralling.
Escalating.
To barbaric proportions.
Reluctantly, we pull the torch to our right:

Red with rage, a Levite stands cutting up a murdered female slave.

This woman has been raped by a gang of Israelites from the tribe of Benjamin.

They abused her all night long (Jud. 19:25).

Then left her to die.

The Levite is cutting the woman up *into twelve parts, limb by limb* (Jud. 19:29), to spread word of this monstrous crime to every tribe of Israel.

Thoroughly disgusted, before long, warriors from all over Israel have descended on the land of Benjamin and declared war. As battles rage, ninety thousand men lose their lives in all. And eventually, with eleven tribes against one, the rest of Israel secures victory over Benjamin.

Every Benjaminite city, and every inhabitant, is burnt to cinders.

Gripping our scalp tight, our hands plough through our hair and fall flat over our face.

Instead of looking outward and spreading peace, Israel has caved in on itself in civil war.

By partnering and aligning with this self-combusting rabble, by trusting in them to spread values of peace, we cannot help but wonder whether Love has in fact made a terrible mistake.

4.02 - It's All About Character

Stirred with compassion and overflowing with affection, a shape of majestic beauty draws close to an elderly man named Samuel, and like a passionate lover wraps over his body. 'They want a king,' Samuel cries until veins protrude through the surface of his skin. 'I'm sorry Yahweh. I'm sorry. *They want a king to rule over us like all the other nations* (1 Sam. 8:5).'

'Samuel, Samuel,' Ruach whispers in pure, golden tones. Though Samuel cannot see his comforter, her presence and voice is unmistakable. '*They have not rejected you. They have rejected me from being their king. They are doing as they have always done. When I took them out of Egypt, they left me and served other gods. They are doing the same to you* (1 Sam. 8:7-8).'

Fully present with Ruach, and yet also watching on from afar, Jesus takes Abba by the hand and says with determination, 'We cannot give up on our children, Father. Look at Samuel. Look at how his heart breaks like ours. We can still do this.'

Deep in thought, Abba nods. 'But should we give them a king?' he asks.

Jesus pauses.

'Oh, Abba, wasn't it great when Gideon declined the opportunity to rule, declaring instead, "Yahweh *will be your ruler*! (Jud. 8:23)" But now... now they have all rejected us. We do not get to speak *to people very often* (1 Sam. 3:1). Anarchy reigns; *everyone* does *what seem*s *right* (Jud. 21:25). These people... they... they need a king.'

'Ruach was with leaders like Samuel, Deborah, Gideon. With our breath inside of them, they ushered in decades of peace for their tribes. A king could do the same for the whole nation, uniting the fragmented tribes, reminding them of our rescue, our Love.'

'Well, we did tell Abraham, "*I will make nations of you, and kings will come from you* (Gen. 17:6)." And other nations, like Edom, have had kings for centuries (Gen. 36:31). It's just that we don't want Israel to be like Edom or any other nation. We want Israel to be *a light to the nations* (Is. 51:4*), influencing Edom.'

'If the king *is a man after* our *own heart* (1 Sam. 13:14*), if the king welcomes Ruach's inspiration, Israel can still stand out. Justice and peace and beauty can still flow through our children's veins.'

'If...' stresses Jesus. 'If... That's the risk. A king could instead ignore Ruach and manipulate the power for his gain. A king could rob and enslave his nation... our nation (1 Sam. 8:17).'

'Character,' Abba says longingly. 'It's all about character.'

Father and Son lock eyes and exchange a proud smile.

Both know that they are united in their choice.

So too is Ruach. '*I will send you a man from the land of Benjamin,*' she tells Samuel, jigging with excitement. '*Appoint him to lead my people. He will save my people from the Philistines. I have seen the suffering of my people, and I have listened to their cry* (1 Sam. 9:16).'

'Son,' says Abba, embracing Jesus so tightly that the two become one. 'We *do not see the same way people see* (1 Sam. 16:7). No human would have chosen a king from the crushed cities of Benjamin, creating the opportunity for beautiful redemption. But Saul is a brilliant choice. He could be a fantastic king. Saul: *there* is *no better Israelite than he* (1 Sam. 9:2).'

Israel's first king paces back and forth with such ferocity and agitation that the grass beneath his feet has withered and browned. So annoyed, so bewildered, so despairing is Saul that his thoughts are roaming wild, rapid and free.

For approaching three decades Saul has reigned over Israel.

Giving his all to the cause.

Winning victories *against Israel's enemies all around* (1 Sam. 14:47).

But for what?

Nothing.

Nothing except criticism.

Silence.

Abandonment.

Rejection.

From God himself.

'"*What pleases* Yahweh *more,*"' Saul mouths bitterly, mocking the verdict passed on to him by Samuel, '"*burnt offerings and sacrifices or obedience to his voice? It is better to obey than to sacrifice... You have rejected* Yahweh*'s command. Now he rejects you as king* (1 Sam. 15:22-23)."'

The outrage, the injustice of it all infuriates Saul to his very core.

Of course, he hasn't been a perfect King. But come on, who would have been? Yes, it was wrong to forbid his army to eat prior to combat. Yes, it was wrong to lie about not killing all the Amalekite's cattle. Yes, it was embarrassing when his armoured Israelites scarpered from the Philistines like little children (1 Sam. 13:7).

But they were Philistines! What more could Saul do against an army that's previously crushed the entire Hittite Empire; against an army with the most formidable weapons around?

Weapons made from iron.

And now the Israelites are locked in the midst of a longstanding stalemate with them. Positioned on either side of a wide reaching valley, neither the Israelites or Philistines can attack without leaving themselves exposed.

Which is why, forty days ago, the Philistines proposed a one-on-one combat. To settle this war once and for all, Israel's best shall take on Philistia's finest, with the winner taking all.

Saul clenches his teeth, in an effort to fight back the tears. He rolls up his fists, and stamps his feet, so as to transmit strength not weakness. For forty days Saul has offered wealth, exemption from taxes, even a wife, in an effort to entice someone into taking up the challenge. But all to no avail.

Though it sickens his heart to acknowledge it, deep down Saul knows that the responsibility should fall upon him. Not only is he King, but Saul also stands physically *a head taller than any other man in Israel* (1 Sam. 9:2).

Day and night the prospect haunts him. The Philistine's challenger, marauding menacingly across the valley, is a three metre tall freak: the giant, Goliath.

Saul sighs: how much longer can he prolong the inevitable?

Prolong the day of his final humiliation.

His crushing disfigurement.

His mangled and bloody end.

Saul rocks his head back and curses aloud. Why should he be forever remembered as the ruler responsible for plunging Israel back into slavery

- a tear finally breaks through Saul's barricaded exterior - as the ruler responsible for reversing the work of Moses' Egyptian liberation?

4.03 - Decapitate His Nemesis

The hanging text before us draws agonisingly to a halt. The cloth is torn, either deliberately ripped, or a victim of the damp. Though the missing fragments may simply be lying beneath our feet, in our eagerness to learn of Saul's fate we jump forward to the text on the next hanging cloth.

What we read steals our breath.

Saul's decapitated body is nailed to the enemy's city walls.

Our head shakes, not quite believing what we are reading.

Saul's armour is on display like a trophy *in the temple of the Ashtoreths* (1 Sam. 31:10), a god of rising popularity throughout the nations.

'No,' we gasp almost inaudibly. 'No. No.'

It cannot be.

The Philistines have conquered Israel.

And the Ashtoreths are lauding victory over Yahweh.

Clutching the lump in our throat, feeling empty and numb, feeling like we have reached the end of the road, we slowly fall to our knees and close our eyes in hopeless disappointment.

Love ripples melodiously from Ruach, Jesus and Abba's every breath, as they draw into the most intimate huddle and form an immeasurable splendour which satisfies an infinity of senses. And united as one, the Lovers choose to journey down into the valley of their vast pain.

'*I am sorry that I made Saul king, because he has stopped following me* (1 Sam. 15:10).'

'We need to find a new king.'

'But is there anyone who still loves us? Anyone who truly - trusts us with their whole life - loves us?'

Ruach's question cracks like a thunderbolt, pinpointing the heart of the Lovers' agony. Silence ensues as the trio bow their heads and hang in the midst of their heartbreak.

When eventually they look back up into each other's eyes, their faces emit solidarity, determination and optimism. 'The new king,' Ruach declares, 'should be someone who has connected with our love for all nations. Listen, my Loves, listen to David on the hills of Bethlehem! Listen to the shepherd boy sing, "Yahweh, *your name is the most wonderful name in all the earth* (Ps. 8:1)," "*the heavens tell the glory of God, and the skies announce what his hands have made* (Ps. 19:1)."'

'Simply stunning. This boy possesses a global perspective because his great-great-grandmother was not an Israelite. She was Rahab, the Canaanite rescued from Jericho.'

'And he is also the great-grandson of Ruth, the Moabite who also chose relationship with us.'

'Oh, Ruth, she was remarkable.' Abba's words are soaked in affection. 'Having lost her husband, her strength in the midst of tragedy, her unswerving commitment...'

'"*Where you go, I will go.*"' Jesus interrupts, quoting Ruth's promise to her mother-in-law Naomi. '"*Where you live, I will live. Your people will be my people, and your God will be my God* (Ruth 1:16)."'

'In an increasingly violent Israel, Ruth's selfless loyalty shone out loud and clear.'

'And now her descendant David burns with the same qualities.'

'Ruach my Love, *go, appoint him, because he is the one* (1 Sam. 16:12).'

As Ruach gives Jesus and Abba a kiss then glides gracefully into the distance, a profound smile stretches across Jesus' cheeks. 'Ruach is on her way to a special, special place. As foreign women in Israel, Rahab and Ruth could potentially have been abused. But in the small town of Bethlehem, they both found sanctuary.'

'Oh Bethlehem, *Bethlehem Ephrathah, though you are too small to be among the army groups from Judah, from you will come one who will rule Israel for me* (Micah 5:2).'

Kneeling within a mattress of cobwebs we open our eyes to find our torch shining down upon a fragment of narrative, presumably fallen from above, presumably outlining action prior to Saul's bloody end:

'*Listen to my cry for help, my King and my God* (Ps. 5:2),' David prays, crouching in pitch-black darkness. '*You will keep us safe; you will always protect us* (Ps. 12:7).'

The look in David's eyes speaks volumes. Here squatting in the depths of a considerable cave is a man whose very survival depends on keeping his wits sharp, on remaining one step ahead of his pursuer.

The pursuer out for his blood.

Yet David's eyes also acknowledge that the net is closing in on him. After all, when his pursuer can summon an entire nation, when his pursuer is Saul, the King of Israel, what chance does he have? At least here, hiding in the desert, David has found some sort of anonymity.

'*Your love is wonderful,*' he sings under his breath, '*Protect me as you would protect your own eye. Hide me under the shadow of your wings. Keep me from the wicked who attack me, from my enemies who surround me (Ps. 17:7-9).*'

Deep down David has hope. Just like his ancestors who spent forty years waiting in the desert, David too is waiting for the fulfilment of a promise from Yahweh; the promise that one day he will be Israel's King.

Suddenly David hears splashing water.

The noise is coming from near the cave's entrance.

David gets to his feet and as he ever so silently creeps forward he draws out his sword; the sword from his most famous victory, the victory which shot David to prominence and ignited Saul's obsessive jealousy; the sword of the formidable Philistine Goliath, who Saul himself was too scared to fight.

The sword used by David to decapitate his nemesis after knocking Goliath down with a single slingshot.

David freezes. What he sees - who he sees - standing in the light of the cave's entrance, causes his heart to pound. Here, urinating against the rocks, alone and exposed before him, is Saul.

This is it, t*oday is the day* Yahweh *spoke of when he said, 'I will give the enemy over to you (1 Sam. 24:4).*'

With one swing of his sword David can save his own life.

Become Israel's King.

And free Israel from Saul's truly abominable reign.

Through David's mind flash images of *men, women, children, babies* (1 Sam. 22:18), all slain, slaughtered, massacred at Saul's orders.

Massacred because of one priest's kindness towards David (1 Sam. 21:1-9).

'*God will ruin you forever,*' David spits, eyeing down the perpetrator of such a gruesome atrocity. '*He will tear you away from the land of the living* (Ps. 52:5).'

One swing of Goliath's sword shall dispense justice.

'KILL HIM,' we shout.

4.04 - Blood On His Hands

Like a sharp jabbing pain, David feels Ruach crying out in his lungs, and immediately his arm snatches, jolting the downward swing of his sword.

The blade clips Saul's robe.

But no more.

David creeps back to the anonymity of his deep dark cave, feeling a huge sense of relief. *There is an old saying: evil things come from evil people* (1 Sam. 24:13). And David - by resisting the urges enflamed within - has refused to repay evil with evil.

Israel's future King has refused to become a murderer.

He has no blood on his hands.

'*I have found in David son of Jesse the kind of man I want* (Acts 13:22),' Abba exclaims, his face shining with joy.

'While most of our children, Abba, are still struggling to adhere to "eye for an eye," David...' Jesus pauses. 'Well, it's as if David has been struck on one cheek, and he has turned to Saul the other (Matt. 5:39).'

'It reminds me of when young David shouted at Goliath, "*You come to me using a sword and two spears. But I come to you in the name of Yahweh All-powerful* (1 Sam. 17:45)." Ever since then his faith has been stretched to its limits. Like Abraham and Moses before him, he has experienced a long arduous ordeal and in the process he has absorbed something of our enduring patience, longing and faith; faith that one day our promises will be fulfilled.'

'With a character like this, now David is ready to be King.'

Still kneeling in a mattress of cobwebs we gather together as many fallen fragments of text as we can find and attempt to piece together the events leading up to Saul's death.

What we discover is so astonishing we can hardly believe it.

Saul's relentless pursuit of David ultimately forced his nemesis to seek refuse in enemy territory; in Philistia, no less. Incredibly, for over a year David swore allegiance to Israel's most formidable foe. Indeed, David built up such respect from the Philistines that when Saul fell on his own sword and Israel finally succumbed to the might of Philistia, the Philistines gave David permission to rule in his home tribe of Judah.

Amazing.

We are in awe at the Rescue Strategists' remarkable achievement.

As we get to our feet with renewed optimism, the light from our torch reveals a corner of the loft much cleaner and tidier than anywhere else. The text on the walls is neatly arranged and undamaged. And in front of the wall, a small bowl sits neatly on a wooden table.

In the bowl there are handfuls of tiny, tiny seeds.

'The Kingdom of heaven is like a mustard seed,' a note by the bowl reads. *'That seed is the smallest of all seeds, but when it grows, it is one of the largest garden plants. It becomes big enough for the wild birds to come and build nests in its branches* (Matt. 13:31).'

'After seven years of David ruling solely in Judah,' the text continues, 'the rest of Israel decides to place their longings for liberation at David's feet. With their resources united together, David leads his Israelites in an uprising against the Philistines and like a mustard seed, from almost nothing, David's dominion grows and grows in size. With the acquisition of highly prized copper and iron, and the capture of key trade routes including ports along the Mediterranean coastline, David's Kingdom quickly becomes a wealthy economic force. Before long, the surrounding nations are seeking refuge in Israel's blossoming branches and David is governor over one of the world's largest Empires.'

Stunned, we lift our hand in the air in celebration.

Out of the blue, here is the news we have been desperately waiting for.

David has completed the mission of Joshua.

Accomplished the rescue of Moses.

And brought respect.

And influence.

To the covenant partner of Yahweh.

Placing Israel in a superb position to play their part in the advancement of Phase Four.

No longer needing to fight off the threat of others, now Israel can finally live out Yahweh's promise to Abraham that *'All the people on earth will be blessed through you* (Gen. 12:3).' Now they can 'love their neighbour

(Lev. 19:18)'; as it says on the wall behind the bowl, now they can 'Love their enemy (Matt. 5:44).'

Indeed, it says that the Rescue Strategist is so delighted by David's achievements that he is ready to lay down another all-important covenant.

We lean forward in anticipation, eager to absorb the full weight of each word from Yahweh to David.

'I will make one of your sons the next king,
And I will set up his kingdom (2 Sam. 7:12).
His family will go on forever.
His kingdom will last before me like the sun.
It will continue forever, like the moon,
Like a dependable witness in the sky (Ps. 89:36-37).'

David's Kingdom will last forever?
Forever?!
Forever!

For the first time in these Headquarters it dawns on us that these ancient narratives might actually be stretching out and connecting to the here and now.

To our life.

To our world.

Which leaves us wondering: three millennia after the life of David, where is David's Kingdom now? Which of his descendants is King?

In the embracing Community of Elohim, Abba bursts into full glorious song:
'Gates, open wide all the way.
  Open wide, aged doors
  So the glorious King will come in.
'Who is this glorious King?
  Yahweh All-powerful -
  He is the glorious King (Ps. 24:7-10).'

The glistening tones of his Father fill Jesus with such pleasure that he cannot suppress the words dancing within him. *'I am the descendant from the family of David,'* (Rev. 22:16) he reveals with elation.

'My beautiful brave Son, the City of David shall open wide its gates and you shall enter in as the euphoric crowds cheer, *"God bless the King of Israel!* (John 12:13)"'

As the sun sets on a warm spring evening, David cannot resist the urges enflamed within him. Bathsheba's stunning figure is just too alluring.

David sleeps with Bathsheba, a married woman.

And Bathsheba becomes pregnant.

Then to cover up his actions, David sends orders for her husband to be killed.

Israel's King becomes a murderer, with blood on his hands.

4.05 - The Dwelling of Yahweh

A murderer and an adulterer, the shame sends David through turmoil. It eats him inside until he falls down on his knees and cries,

'God, be merciful to me,
Take away my sin, and I will be clean.
Wash me, and I will be whiter than snow.
...Create in me a pure heart.
...Give me back the joy of your salvation
...Save me from the guilt of murder (Ps. 51:1-14).'

And for the rest of his days David sings of the forgiveness he found embedded at the heart of Yahweh's Rescue Mission. He longs for his lyrics to spread throughout Israel's extensive Empire. He prays that they awaken the world to this God who forgives.

To this God *who shows mercy and is kind,*
Who doesn't *become angry quickly,*
Who has *great love and faithfulness* (Ps. 86:15).
Who does not demand harrowing sacrifices, even child sacrifices.
Because *the sacrifice God wants is a broken spirit,*
...a heart that is broken and sorry for sin (Ps. 51:17).
David sings in faith and eager anticipation:

'Lord, all the nations you have made
Will come and worship you (Ps. 86:9).'

Surrounded full-circle by absolute splendour, the King of Israel can hardly breathe, let alone move. Solomon, the son of David and Bathsheba, is held transfixed, mesmerised by the sheer extent of the beauty directly ahead of him.

Solomon feels like a child immersed in a story, gazing into another world. Only this world is actual, factual, real, physical, here, now, glistening in the finest gold, brimming in meticulously crafted bronze. This is a world like none ever seen before; a vista more elegant, more magnificent, more heart-stopping than even the great pyramids of Egypt; a piece of heaven on earth, a creation fit for the Creator, a house ready for the dwelling of Yahweh.

If only his father David were here to see this; he would be so proud. David had worked tirelessly in preparation for this day, modelling his plans on the Tabernacle of Moses, acquiring all the stone, iron, and cedar wood needed for construction (1 Chron. 22:2-4).

Yet David had been forbidden from building the Temple in his lifetime; the Temple which David believed was advancing one of Yahweh's deepest desires. Solomon's father had *fought many wars* and *killed many people* (1 Chron. 22:8), and Yahweh did not want the foundations of Yahweh's residence on Earth to be war and bloodshed.

But peace and unity.

By the time David died, Israel was at peace with its enemies. Free from the fear of attack, Solomon - whose very name means 'peace' - has governed over a society flourishing in creativity and discovery, productivity and development, travel and trade, education and literature, music and art.

Solomon's reign has also benefited from a legacy of unity left by his father. David helped quell a sense that his own tribe Judah was superior, by moving his capital city away from Judah into recently captured territory. High on a hill and visible for miles around, Jerusalem was a city that the whole of Israel could be proud of.

It was emblematic of Israel's fresh start.

Symptomatic of their expansion into the largest Empire on Earth.

Now the opening of this Temple in Jerusalem will further unite Solomon's nation.

Around their shared history.

And common purpose.

This Temple shall stand as a permanent, inescapable reminder of Yahweh's desired intimacy with Israel.

'If you obey all my laws and commands,' Yahweh told Solomon, *'I will do for you what I promised your father David. I will live among the Israelites in this Temple, and I will never leave my people Israel* (1 Kings 6:12-13).'

If.

If.

If you obey.

The words have vibrated through Solomon like a clanging cymbal, reminding him of his nation's repeated neglect of the laws given to Moses.

Taking their luxury for granted at one point they even lost the wooden box that Yahweh's commandments were kept in.

Which is why, Solomon's heart is pounding as he watches Levite priests carrying the rescued and recovered Ark of the Covenant into the heart of the Temple, restoring it to its rightful place in the Holy of Holies.

All of a sudden the entire Temple is encompassed within a mighty swirling cloud as Ruach dances and sprints and soars, enveloping all within the Shekinah, the visible presence of Yahweh.

God's people are in his presence (1 Kings 7:48).

Solomon is no longer frozen to the spot. He is spinning around with arms raised high, feeling as if he is flying; as if he has taken hold of Ruach's hand and he is soaring through the Temple with her. The love he feels is like none he has ever experienced before. This love is uncomplicated, uncluttered, a love with no ulterior motive.

And for the first time in his life Solomon truly appreciates the desire for exclusivity in relationship. At last he grasps why Yahweh's first command to Israel was, *'You must not have any other gods except me* (Ex. 20:3).' And why, why would anyone choose any other god - a god present only in lumps of wood chiselled by man - when Yahweh is like this?

Alive.

Near.

Tangible.

Visible.

Soothing.

Exhilarating.

'Yahweh, *I have truly built a wonderful temple for you - a place for you to live forever* (1 Kings 8:13).' The raw and genuine emotion throughout Solomon's announcement stops Ruach in her tracks. The Shekinah hovers over Solomon, utterly captivated by his words, words spoken as if Solomon is conversing with a lifelong friend.

'*People who are not Israelites,*' the king continues, '*foreigners from other lands, will hear about your greatness and power. They will come from far away to pray at this Temple* (1 Kings 8:41-42).'

'Jerusalem, you are the foundations of peace,' Jesus replies, speaking as a Groom caressing his Bride, 'you are the light of the world, a city *on a hill* that *cannot be hidden* (Matt. 5:14).'

The Community of Elohim spin head over heels, dizzy with exhilaration. And when the Queen of Sheba travels for many months to see Solomon's Temple for herself, when she concludes, '*Praise* Yahweh *your God... Yahweh has constant love for Israel* (1 Kings 10:9),' their faces shine with delight.

Until.

Until mouths drop in shock.

And horror.

And devastated sorrow.

When *on a hill east of Jerusalem, Solomon* builds *two places for worship.*

One for *Chemosh, the hated god of the Moabites.*

The other for *Molech, the hated god of the Ammonites* (1 Kings 11:7).

4.06 - After the Affair

'Ahhhh, Solomon,' we scream at the top of our voice. 'Solomon, Solomon, what are you doing? If the Shekinah of Yahweh was indeed so real, so alive, so near, tangible and visible, soothing and exhilarating, why, why would you build shrines to other gods? Solomon, you idiot!'

In the midst of the silence, staring helplessly into the dark, the severity of our own reaction takes us by surprise. Why do we feel such anger? It's not as if Solomon's actions are affecting us, are they?

But as the minutes pass there is no shaking off our sorrow. Bewildered and confused, our head rocks in frustration. And for the first time in this mysterious Headquarters we notice our hunger and thirst. It must be hours since we last ate or drank anything. Our thoughts turn to the comfort of home. Our eyes close, our shoulders ease, our head drops.

But Solomon.

Solomon you idiot.

What are you doing?

We snap to attention.

What are we doing? We cannot leave. Not now. Not after what Solomon has just done. Our focus returns to the wall only to find the narrative covered over by another piece of paper, paper that looks like it has been torn from elsewhere.

What we read on the additional text is so shocking it freezes us rigid. God tells a man named Hosea, *'Go and marry an unfaithful woman and have unfaithful children... because the people in this country have been completely unfaithful to* me (Hosea 1:2).'

This is chilling.

Unnerving.

Heart-wrenching.

Hosea is being asked to whole-heartedly and exclusively commit himself to a prostitute, a woman who is highly likely to not return his affection, a woman who will carry on sleeping around with other men. And why? Because this woman's constant betrayal of Hosea illustrates Israel's unfaithfulness towards Yahweh.

'My people ask wooden idols for advice,' says Yahweh,

'They ask those sticks of wood to advise them!
Like prostitutes, they have chased after other gods
And have left their own God (Hosea 4:12).'

Israel has been like a married prostitute. And whenever Hosea returns home to find his wife in bed with another man, he will be sharing in the heartbreak that Yahweh feels.

Oh, Solomon, Solomon, what are you doing?

Solomon, you are being unfaithful to Yahweh.

Solomon, you are sleeping around with other gods.

Solomon, you are acting like your Father when he met your Mother.

Solomon, you are having an affair.

Perhaps the anger that we feel, perhaps that's something of God's anger. After all, it's not like Yahweh hasn't been betrayed before. When the golden calf was built at the foot of Mount Sinai, when it was announced, *'Israel, these are your gods who brought you out of Egypt (Ex. 32:4),'* God was so heartbroken his fury killed three thousand people.

What will the consequences be this time?

We tear off the page on Hosea, and tentatively peer beneath.

The consequence of the affair soon becomes clear.

After the affair, comes the break up.

The break-up of Israel.

The nation splits into two.

'I will tear your kingdom *away from your son when he becomes king,'* Yahweh tells Solomon. *'I will not tear away all the kingdom from him, but I will leave him one tribe to rule. I will do this because of David, and because of Jerusalem, the city I have chosen* (1 Kings 11:11-13).'

Because of David.

We recall that when David faced up to the consequences of his affair with Bathsheba, he was spurred on to bring peace to his dominion. Solomon on the other hand seems to have turned a blind eye to severe discontentment festering throughout his nation. By the time his son Rehoboam takes to the throne, Israel is - as predicted - on the brink of revolution.

Across Israel, in all regions except David's home tribe of Judah and areas surrounding Judah, the people cry, *'We have no share in David!* (1 Kings 12:16)'* Allegiance shifts to a man named Jeroboam and they hail him as King.

In terms of size, economic prowess and military potential, Jeroboam's dominion is the only Israel worthy of note. To the rest of the world, it is the only desirable ally. All Rehoboam's region really has in its favour is the city of Jerusalem and its Temple.

But not having Jerusalem's Temple within his borders does pose a major problem for Jeroboam's Israel: where will they worship?

And more to the point, who will they worship? Having broken away from David's grandson, Jeroboam can hardly now endorse a god with an everlasting commitment to David's family, can he?

Jeroboam needs to find a new god for Israel, and fast.

So in the north and south of his nation, Jeroboam builds a golden calf. And announces: '*Israel, here are your gods who brought you out of Egypt* (1 Kings 12:28).'

Ruach, Jesus and Abba bury their heads into each other's chests. With pain shooting through their hearts they find solace in their perfect community of unfaltering Love.

'*My people have made up their minds to turn away from me,*' says Jesus, choking through his tears. '*Oh, Israel, how can I give you up? How can I give you away, Israel? My heart beats for you* (Hosea 11:7-8).' Israel *put on her rings and jewellery, and went chasing after her lovers, but she forgot me!* (Hosea 2:13)'

'Oh Beautiful Jesus, my Love, soon the prostitute will be drawn to you and her love for us shall overflow. She will kiss your feet and wash them with her tears. She shall douse them with perfume and dry them with her hair (Luke 7:36).'

Abba nods. 'Hosea's name literally means "Rescue". We will ask Hosea to pay money to rescue and buy back his wife, the prostitute, from her other lovers. *In the same way* I love *the people of Israel* (Hosea 3:1). *I will forgive them for leaving me and will love them freely* (Hosea 14:4).'

Jesus looks up, his eyes shining romantically.

'*I will make* Israel *my promised bride forever* (Hosea 2:19). I will pay the price to restore her purity, and buy back her beauty. And *in the future she will call me "my husband* (Hosea 2:16).'"

4.07 - Like Wild Animals

Naked and skinny and covered in flies, a group of young children clamber on top of a rubbish dump, scavenging through the filth, desperate to discover discarded scraps of meat, desperate to feed off their findings.

From the other side of the road, Amos watches the scene stunned to his core.

Heartbroken that humans could live like this.

Dumbfounded that nobody else seems to care.

He may only be a shepherd from the gentle countryside of Judah, but Amos has never seen poverty like this.

Yet when he turns to his right, the sight couldn't be more contrasting. Never has Amos seen wealth like this. Back home in Judah, all this extravagance would be unimaginable, let alone unattainable.

Amos is standing as a foreigner in Bethel, the southernmost town in Israel, famous for Jeroboam's golden calf. The statue may be a century and a half old but it is still as popular as ever. Every day thousands of worshippers bow down before the calf, thanking their gods for their luxury, for their meat and wine, for their palaces decked in ivory, for lounging around (Amos 6:4-6), for security and safety.

For being untouchable.

The gods of Baal have been kind and generous.

They are worthy of praise.

Amos turns back to the children covered in dirt, scavenging like wild animals.

How is this possible?

Poverty.

Extreme poverty.

Next to extreme luxury.

How?

Now Amos understands the frightening tone of Yahweh's voice, the day his life was turned upside down.

It was furious.

Livid.

Disgusted.

Sickened.

Repulsed.

Amos shudders. He whimpers nervously. Now it is his job to tell Bethel everything that Yahweh said. And they are not going to like it. The Israelites will condemn him as a madman and arrest him as a criminal. Why should a quiet, peaceful, respected shepherd deserve a fate like that?

Amos catches the eye of an abandoned child, scratched and bruised. He takes a deep breath as the heat stirs in his heart. It swells and swells until the child holds out his hand begging for food, and Amos can hold it in no longer. Amos screams out in agony.

Stunned passers-by turn their heads.

Then Amos lets fly.

'This is what Yahweh *says: "For the many crimes of Israel, I will punish them. For silver, they sell people that have done nothing wrong; they sell the poor as if they were nothing, and they refuse to be fair to those that are suffering.*

'Listen to this funeral song that I sing about you, people of Israel (Amos 5:1). *You turn justice upside down, and you throw on the ground what is right (Amos 5:7). You walk on poor people, forcing them to give you grain (Amos 5:11)."'*

Already Bethel's streets are in uproar.

From the onslaught of abuse, one shout stuns Amos more than any other: 'You hypocrite! You Judean hypocrite!'

Amos stops because he knows it is true: he is a Judean hypocrite. Judah is just as guilty of abusing the poor as Israel. Indeed, the very origins of Israel's breakaway from Judah were rooted in King Solomon's tyranny and his point-blank hypocrisy.

With his mouth Solomon would say, *'The rich and poor are alike -* Yahweh *made them all* (Prov. 22:2)'; *'whoever mistreats the poor insults their Maker* (Prov. 17:5)'; *'being kind to the poor is like lending to* Yahweh (Prov. 19:17).'

But in practice, Solomon sentenced vast portions of his nation to decades of compulsory back-breaking labour (1 Kings 9:15). The builders of Solomon's ambitious constructions were treated as if they were slaves in Egypt, building Pharaoh's pyramids.

'Remember you were slaves in Egypt,' (Deut. 24:18) Moses used to implore his liberated Israelites. But Solomon forgot Moses' plea. He forgot Israel's call to fight for equality, to stand up for those who are suffering.

When Jeroboam challenged Solomon's successor over the oppression, Rehoboam's response echoed that of Egypt's Pharaoh when first confronted by Moses. Rehoboam simply made the suffering worse. *'My father beat you with whips,'* Rehoboam sneered, *'but my whips shall be tipped with metal (1 Kings 12:14).'*

It was revolting.

And Jeroboam was left with no choice but to revolt.

The nation of Israel split in two.

'Listen to me,' Amos continues. *'Listen, you who walk on helpless people, saying, "we can charge them more and give them less, and we can change the scales to cheat the people. We will buy poor people for silver and needy people for the price of a pair of sandals (Amos 8:2-6)."*

'Listen! Come to Yahweh and live, or he will move like fire against the descendants of Joseph. The fire will burn Bethel, and there will be no one to put it out (Amos 5:6).'

As the crowds explode with laughter and the authorities lead Amos away, as Amos struggles and screams, *'Yahweh says, "I will destroy Israel from off the Earth! ... I am giving the command to scatter the nation of Israel among all the nations (Amos 9:8),"'* little does anyone realise that out in the east an Empire is on the rise.

An Empire with eyes set on world domination.

An Empire rampaging ravenously, spilling and spraying blood at will.

An Empire so large that even Israel in David's glory days was miniscule by comparison.

The Assyrian Empire: stretching as far east as Babylonia, taking in the mighty Tigris and Euphrates Rivers, and now with its sights set on conquering Egypt in the west.

And to get to Egypt, Assyria must first conquer Israel.

When the enemy finally arrives at Israel's borders, the nation is a political shambles.

Murder after murder has left Israel with five kings in ten years.

The Assyrians slay their prey with consummate ease.

Like a lion devouring a lamb, Israel is ripped to shreds.

Those left alive are enslaved and deported, scattered across the far-reaches of Assyria's Empire. Their collective identity torn apart, the exiles quickly fade into obscurity.

In the Law of Moses the ultimate punishment for repeated unrepentant disobedience was to *'rot away in their enemies' countries* (Lev. 26:39).'

And that is what happens.

Israel is no more.

All that remains of the nation fathered and established by Abraham, Jacob, Moses and David is tiny Judah.

The Rescue Mission is hanging by a thread.

And the bloodthirsty Assyrians are licking their lips.

Judah shall be their easiest conquest yet.

4.08 - Dead

The sky hangs heavy and grey over Jerusalem, the rain powers down. And in the courtyard of Solomon's Temple one solitary prisoner suspends shackled and shamed, head and hands locked in the stocks, blood seeping from his searing wounds. Propelled by the relentless rain, the blood skims down his cold naked body. In his mind the prisoner has given up living. Jeremiah would rather be dead.

"'*Perhaps they will listen* (Jer. 26:2),'" Jeremiah snaps furiously, bitterness and sarcasm scratching his throat. "'Perhaps you can save them," you told me. But I never stood a chance, did I Yahweh? My mission was doomed from the start.

'*Can a leopard change its spots? In the same way, Jerusalem… cannot change and do good. They are accustomed to doing evil* (Jer. 13:23). They are addicted to it.

'Yahweh, *you tricked me* and *I have become a joke* (Jer. 20:7). Why?' Jeremiah screeches. '*Why did I ever come out of the womb to see trouble and sorrow and to end my days in shame? (Jer. 20:18*) I don't understand why my pain has no end* (Jer. 15:18). *I wish my head were like a spring of water and my eyes like a fountain of tears! Then I could cry day and night for my people who have been killed* (Jer. 9:1).

'When Judah was surrounded by the Assyrians, when they were running out of food and it looked certain that they'd be defeated, oh, of course, they cared about you then, Yahweh. Of course, they were grateful for you when you went and decimated the Assyrian camp, killing hundreds of thousands overnight.

"'*For the sake of David* (2 Kings 19:34),'" you rescued them from imminent extinction.

'And it couldn't have been more dramatic.

'More memorable.

'But in a flash they forget you. They only care about you, Yahweh, when it suits them, when they need you. When Jerusalem is surrounded and extinction seems imminent, oh of course, they remember you then. Then they remember your covenant with David.

'They remember that covenant, Yahweh, because it's unconditional. They think it promises that David's kingdom - their kingdom - will go on forever. They think it guarantees them rescue from every enemy.

'But they forget your conditional covenant, Yahweh. The one you made with Moses, where you gave us a task, a responsibility, appointing us to usher in your kingdom of peace over all the earth.

'Obedience promised prosperity.

'Disobedience: destruction.

'Oh, Yahweh, I'm so sorry... if only I could have stopped Josiah from fighting the Egyptians... it was all going so well; Josiah had found the lost book of Moses' laws in the Temple, dusted it down and Judah had recommitted to your ways. The Assyrian stranglehold on Judean culture was weakening, freeing Josiah to smash the statues of their gods, like Hezekiah had done. He even tore down Jeroboam's golden calf in Bethel.

'But then...' Another wave of weeping overcomes Jeremiah, '...then Josiah was killed.

'Killed by the Egyptians.

'And now our King is in an alliance with the Pharaoh.

'We are slaves of Egypt once again.'

Jeremiah raises his eyes to the Temple, Solomon's famous triumphant masterpiece.

'I'm sorry, Yahweh... *this place where* you *have chosen to be worshipped is nothing more than a hideout for robbers* (Jer. 7:11). It is filled with altars to Egyptian gods. Yahweh, it must break your heart. *Judah saw that* you *divorced unfaithful Israel because of her adultery* (Jer. 3:8) yet still we sleep around with other gods.

'And soon we will be trying to please the Egyptian gods...,' Jeremiah chokes, overwhelmed by inconsolable grief, '...soon we will be offering the gods our own children.

'Swords slice limbs.

'Smoke chokes lungs.

'Flames char flesh.

'The limbs, lungs and flesh of innocent, screaming children.

'Even the King of Judah will feel compelled to tie up his own son, pull down his knife and watch his flesh and blood go up in flames.

'Just like King Manasseh did (2 Kings 21:6).

'Just like King Ahaz (2 Kings 16:3).'

We stand frozen rigid, totally stunned. Then, as the horror sinks in, we kick out in rage, slamming our foot into a rafter of the loft causing the whole roof to shudder and a foul, dank cloud of dust to shower down on our head.

Child sacrifice! This is horrendous. Child sacrifice was supposed to have been eradicated from the earth centuries ago? That's why God allowed the Israelites to massacre the Canaanites.

Yet still the ghastly slaughters go on. Even the King of Jerusalem, God's city of peace, God's light to the world, ties up his own son... a tear drips from our chin. How could humans have got it so wrong?

When God stopped Abraham from sacrificing Isaac, when God told Moses that only animals should ever be offered as a sacrifice, didn't he get the message across clearly enough?

Love hates the burning of children.

The Canaanites were destroyed for these crimes.

And Judah deserves to die too.

But Judah won't be destroyed, will it?

God saved them from the Assyrians and he will do it again.

No matter how fierce the enemy surrounding it, no matter how much Jerusalem deserves destruction, Love - long suffering, enduring Love - will protect his city on a hill.

We are convinced: David's kingdom will last forever.

It's covenanted.

It's contracted.

'For the sake of David': that's what's keeping the Rescue Mission alive.

A Temple guard steps out into the rain, strides over to his prisoner and to shut up Jeremiah's constant chattering, strikes him hard across the face.

Jeremiah riles and spits then slowly lifts his head and glares into his torturer's unrepentant eyes. *'Run for your lives!'* Jeremiah chokes, gasping for every breath. *'Disaster is coming* (Jer. 6:1-2).'

Love's covenant partner, Love's representative on earth, has committed *more evil than the nations* Yahweh *destroyed ahead of the Israelites* (2 Kings 21:9).

Leaving Love with no other option (Jer. 9:7).

The Babylonians surround Jerusalem.

The embracing Elohim roars out in excruciating agony.
And the enemy breaks through Jerusalem's barricades.
Swords slice limbs.
Smoke chokes lungs.
Flames char flesh.
Man, woman or child, the Babylonians kill at will.

First the words blur then the wall sways.
The Rescue Mission, it's all over.
It's finished.
Dead.
All that work, all that blood, sweat and tears - Noah, Abraham, Moses, David - it's all come to nothing. Our eyes glaze over and we stumble back, arms swinging chaotically. Seeing nothing, feeling nothing but pain, we trip and, as if unconscious and fainting, crash to the dusty loft floor.
Yet still we fall.
Flying, flailing, falling through the air.
Flying.
Flailing.
Falling.
Until slam; flat solid concrete knocks us cold.

4.09 - The Rejected Romantic

We can hear the screams.

We can see the devastation.

Tripping between blackouts and flashes of white, we see the smoke and ash swirling in the massacre's aftermath, the shrapnel and debris flying in the wind, holding no regard for the mutilated bodies in the rubble below.

'My eyes have no more tears and I am sick to the stomach. I feel empty inside because my people have been destroyed (Lam. 2:10-12). *Jerusalem once was a great city among the nations, but now she is like a widow* (Lam. 1:1), a widow who has been stripped naked (Ez. 16:37).'

Our vision is blurring, fading to black, but the voice is crystal clear.

A second voice, broken and choking, interjects: *'The babies are so thirsty their tongues stick to the roofs of their mouths. Children beg for bread, but no one gives them any. Those who once ate fine foods are now starving in the streets* (Lam. 4:4-5). *With their own hands kind women cook their own children* (Lam. 4:10).'

We are devoid of our senses, conscious of nothing but the voices.

'No longer could I share David's Temple with all their other lovers. I had to leave our home (Ez. 10:18), leave her unprotected, exposed, vulnerable. Now *the stones of the Temple are scattered at every street corner* (Lam. 4:1). Passers-by laugh, *"Is this the city the people called the most beautiful city, the happiest place on earth?* (Lam. 2:15)"'

The sound of a third voice awakens our senses. It is gorgeous and diverse, shimmering like a rainbow. Suddenly our entire body feels like it is on fire.

'The happiest place on earth, Jerusalem was our heaven on earth, the start of Eden's restoration, paradise's rescue. Now Jerusalem is a hell; a hell like Gehenna, the Valley of Hennom, the graveyard of children slaughtered *as sacrifices for Molech* (Jer. 32:35).'

We cannot move a muscle. We imagine the three mourners in floods of tears, locked in embrace.

'"*What can I bring before* Yahweh?"' our Bride asks. "*Should I give my first child for the evil I have done? Should I give my very own child for my sin?* (Micah 6:6-7)" No, no, no, my love, why, why, why, would we seek death and bloodshed? We are not like the gods of the human imagination. We desire life. We want you to *do what is right to other people, love being kind to others, and live humbly, obeying your God* (Micah 6:8). *Let justice roll on like a river, righteousness like a never-failing stream!* (Amos 5:24)'

'There is only one way, Abba, to open eyes to the truth that humans don't need to kill their children as sacrifices. There needs to be an ultimate sacrifice, a definitive death which defeats *the power of sin just once - enough for all time* (Rom. 6:10).'

A quivering silence ensues in which we finally manage to open our eyes and establish that we are lying stretched out on a cold, concrete floor.

'*On the day you were born...*'

The floor is littered with debris, the aftermath of a considerable crash: our crash.

'*...you were thrown out into the open field, because you were hated. When I passed by and saw you kicking about in your blood, I said to you, "Live!" You grew up and became tall and became like a beautiful jewel.*'

Each word feels like it is being forced out under tremendous strain.

'*Later when I passed by you and looked at you, I saw that you were old enough for love. So I spread my robe over you and covered your nakedness. I also made a promise to you and entered into an agreement with you so that you became mine* (Ez. 16:6-8).

'*I wrapped you in fine linen and covered you with silk. I put jewellery on you: bracelets on your arms, a necklace round your neck, a ring in your nose, earrings in your ears and a beautiful crown on your head.*'

The words are flowing more easily now. And we lie mesmerised.

'*You were very beautiful and became a queen. Then you became famous among the nations, because you were so beautiful* (Ez. 16:9-14).'

The intimacy.

The romance.

It only adds to the tragedy.

The tragedy of the Rescue Mission's failure.

'You *took your beautiful jewellery... and you made for yourselves male idols so you could be a prostitute with them... You gave my oil and incense as an offering to them* (Ez. 16:17-18).'

The beautiful Bride, crowned as a queen, chose instead to be a prostitute.

Tears dripping to the floor, we can do nothing but simply lie in the agony. We surrender to the poetry of Love, the emotion of the Rejected Romantic.

'You also took your sons and daughters who were my children, and you sacrificed them to the idols as food. You killed my children and offered them up in fire (Ez. 16:20-21). *I never commanded you to do such a hateful thing. It never entered my mind that you would* (Jer. 32:35).'

The pain is just too much. We long to be numb again. We screw our eyes shut and our mind trips back to Gehenna, the Valley of Hennom, the graveyard of bones left drying and decaying in the midday sun.

'Valley of dry bones,' says the rainbow voice, '*I will put muscles on you and flesh on you and cover you with skin. Then I will put breath in you so you will come to life* (Ez. 37:5). *I will put my Spirit inside you and help you* (Ez. 36:27). *You will live in the land I gave to your ancestors, and you will be my people, and I will be your God* (Ez. 36:28). You *will say,* "*This land was ruined, but now it has become like the Garden of Eden* (Ez. 36:35)."'

'From the graveyard of Gehenna to the Garden of Eden, yes Ruach my love, creation can still be restored. Our separation will only be temporary; soon we will live with our Bride forever in marital bliss.'

'But love remains a choice.

'Who will want this bliss? Who will choose it?'

Without a moment's hesitation, we respond: 'We will. We will.'

Steadily, the ash and rubble in our mind's eye transforms into a landscape of rolling hills and rivers. And basking in the panorama of paradise a new breath, a new spirit rushes through us.

And brings us life.

4.10 - The Roaring Lion

Under the full force of the lion's roar, Daniel's elderly bones feel as if they will shatter. Pinned against the wall, he fights to stay hidden in the dark, fights to slow the beat of his heart and quiet the fear in his breath. The roar is still ricocheting through Daniel's body when he hears the sound that he fears the most.

The sound of a lion rising.

Prowling.

Approaching.

It is not possible for Daniel to push himself back any further into the wall.

First he feels the breath, then the whiskers and mane brushing across his face.

'*I will be like a lion to Israel,*' Yahweh told Hosea, '*I will attack them and tear them to pieces* (Hosea 5:14).' Now Daniel is standing face to face with Yahweh: Yahweh the roaring lion, destroyer of Jerusalem; the lion who ripped the meat from his lambs.

'*My God, my God, why have you rejected me* (Ps. 22:1)?' Daniel silently weeps. Screwing up his face, bracing himself for the moment the lion's jaws rip apart his sagging flesh, Daniel dispenses one final frantic prayer.

'Yahweh *is my shepherd* (Ps. 23:1).

Yahweh *is my shepherd.*'

A wet slobbery tongue slides across Daniel's face: the taste before the bite.

'Yahweh *is my shepherd.*

'Yahweh *is my shepherd.*'

Another giant lick.

'Yahweh's *love never ends* (Lam. 3:22).

'Yahweh's *love never ends.*

'He *will not reject his people for ever* (Lam. 3:31).

'He *does not like to punish people* (Lam. 3:33).'

Daniel dares to open up his senses. There is no excruciating pain. He has not been torn into a hundred mutilated pieces. And he can hear the sound of the lion retreating; to Daniel's immeasurable relief, for now he has been spared.

Daniel sits down on the ground, clutching his knees close to his chest for warmth. As minutes turn to hours through the night, Daniel's thoughts focus upon the words of hope embedded in the hearts of every Judean exile in Babylon.

'*Babylon will be powerful for seventy years.*' Yahweh promises in the scrolls of Jeremiah. 'But then *I will come to you* and *bring you back to Jerusalem* (Jer. 29:10).'

And the seventy years are nearly up.

Rescue is imminent.

Already the Babylonian Empire is crumbling.

Already Babylon's king is Median not Babylonian.

Already Jehoiachin, the heir to Judah's throne, has been released from prison (2 Kings 25:27). Soon Jerusalem's exiles will be returning home.

Seventy years ago it looked as if Yahweh had left his people forever. '*Where is your God?*' (Ps. 42:3) the Babylonian captors would laugh, pointing at Jerusalem's decimated Temple.

But this was not divorce, only separation.

Even during the most widespread massacre, the stripped naked Bride was still given an opportunity to choose life. According to Jeremiah, those who surrendered without fighting would not die but would '*escape with their lives and live* (Jer. 38:2).'

And live they have.

Here in Babylon, the Judeans have prospered so much as bankers and merchants, working within a thriving global metropolis of trade, Daniel had even begun to wonder whether Yahweh was actually still with the exiles, helping them in Babylon.

But that wasn't possible, was it?

The gods are fixed to certain locations, aren't they?

One god rules here.

Another god rules there.

Marduk has Babylon.

Yahweh has - had - Jerusalem.

That's just how it is.

But when Daniel and some other Judean exiles began to hear Yahweh speak to them in Babylon, entire worldviews began to crumble.

One exile even heard Yahweh promise the Judeans, *'When you walk through fires, you will not be burnt* (Is. 43:2).' And sure enough, when Hananiah, Mishael and Azariah were thrown into an enormous blazing furnace, incredibly, miraculously, *their hair was not burned, their robes were not burned and they did not even smell of smoke* (Dan. 3:26). What's more, a mysterious fourth figure was seen standing with them in the flames.

Leaving Daniel in no doubt: Yahweh was with them.

In Babylon.

In Marduk's Babylon.

'I am the true God,' the exiles heard Yahweh proclaim. *'There was no God before me, and there will be no God after me* (Is. 43:10).'

The exiles couldn't believe their ears.

The thought was mind-blowing.

It was the greatest ground-breaking revelation of all.

But bit by bit by bit, it began to make sense.

Yahweh is not limited to one location, because Yahweh is not limited at all. Yahweh can be both the shepherd and the lion, or both the father and the husband, or the mother unable to *forget the baby she nurses* (Is. 49:15).

Because Yahweh is the first God and the last God.

The one and only God.

Daniel stretches out his legs and marvels once more at the thought of one giant God who *rules over every kingdom on earth* (Dan. 5:21), a God who created the entire world peacefully, who simply spoke and there was.

If only the Babylonians knew this too then perhaps they wouldn't be so violent. They think that Marduk created the world by ripping apart his rival Tiamet then added humans to the earth to be his slaves, to do the work that the gods didn't want to.

Daniel rests his head down to the ground. He rests in the knowledge that the one true God has invited all humans to work in relationship with their Creator, sharing responsibility for the cultivation of creation. But as the hours pass Daniel makes no effort to still his racing mind. Daniel may know that he has been created in the image of Love, but how can he sleep when he is still a lamb lying by lions?

'Daniel, I love you,' Ruach whispers, nursing the restless babe in her arms. 'Thank you for not fighting back, thank you for surrendering without violence. The path you have chosen is the only way - the only way to bring peace to earth.

'Beautiful Daniel, my love, *I will not forget you. I have written your name on my hand* (Is. 49:15-16). *Forget what happened before, and do not think about the past. Look at the new thing I am going to do* (Is. 43:18-19). *For a long time I have kept silent, I have been quiet and held myself back. But now, like a woman in childbirth, I cry out, I gasp, I pant* (Is. 42:14*).

'The shepherd will return to his scattered lambs and lead his flock home. Then the lion will become a lamb.'

4.11 - Completing Phase Four

What?

No, no, this can't be right.

Only a few minutes ago, we had felt new life, a new breath rushing through our body. With only a few pages attached to the otherwise blank Phase Four wall, we had felt confident that these texts would bring a positive conclusion to our painful journey through the Headquarters' loft.

But now we read that the Persians have conquered the Babylonians. And stretching from India to Egypt, the Persian Empire is the largest world superpower yet. Worse still, throughout Persia, swords are being prepared for massacre; an order has been given *to destroy, kill and completely wipe out all* Judeans, *young and old, women and little children too* (Est. 3:13).

This is wrong.

God had promised the Judeans restoration.

A return to Jerusalem.

Not massacre.

But no: the lion is clearly still roaring. And we do not want to go through all that agony again.

We skip ahead to the final text on the wall.

We just want to know how this ends.

Nehemiah's imagination is running wild: so amazing is this scene before him that Yahweh must be smiling, grinning, singing, even dancing. To Nehemiah's left is Jerusalem's rebuilt Temple; to his right, the renovated city walls. And straight ahead of him, every resident of Jerusalem stands in mesmeric hush in the Temple courtyard, listening to Ezra read aloud the laws Yahweh gave to Moses.

Everyone in the crowd has their own personal tale of liberation and restoration to tell, but one family in particular catches Nehemiah's eye. Until recently, this family had been so crippled by poverty they had been forced to sell their children as slaves (Neh. 5:5), just to make ends meet.

Now the family stands reunited.

Nehemiah smiles: this is what happens when Yahweh's instructions in the Laws of Moses are actually followed. These laws may be one thousand years old but they still have the potential to literally, physically, set people free (Lev. 25:41).

To bring equality.

To end poverty.

And offer a fresh start for all.

By cutting extortionate taxes, slashing the interest charged on debts (Neh. 5:7) and announcing a day of Jubilee where all slaves are declared free (Lev. 25:40), Nehemiah and Ezra have brought a piece of heaven back to earth. At long last Amos' cry for justice has been heard.

The new breath within us flickers with excitement. And sheer delight. Our hopes for Phase Four's conclusion had been well placed after all. But how, we wonder? How did the Judeans' fate transform from imminent extinction to renewal in Jerusalem, in such a short space of time?

It all begins with a wife sitting her husband down for a voluptuous banquet.

It begins with the Queen of Persia revealing a secret.

As the Judean extermination date edges ever closer, the most powerful woman in the world takes a deep breath and puts her life on the line.

Queen Esther reveals her true identity.

She is herself Judean.

The King is silenced.

For many minutes he just sits sipping his wine, breathing in its aroma, and staring at the most beautiful woman he has ever seen, his picture of perfection. This woman's sensational eyes never fail to slip behind the walls of his kingly exterior. Esther reminds him that he is human.

'My king,' continues Esther, authoritative yet flirtatious, 'if you are pleased with me, and if it pleases you, let me live. This is what I ask. And let my people live too (Est. 7:3).'

In an instant, the Rescue Mission is transformed.

Esther's courageous confession ushers in a *time of happiness, joy, gladness and honour for the Jewish people* (Est. 8:15). It paves the way for her cousin and adopted father to be crowned the second most powerful man in the whole of Persia (Est. 10:3). It inspires Persia's next

King, Esther's own stepson, to encourage both Ezra and Nehemiah to return to Jerusalem and restore the city's former glory.

And it prompts m*any people through all the empire* to become *Jews* (Est. 8:17).

They may not be Judean.

But they choose to honour the Judean God.

Remarkable.

The Israelites have continuously rejected their commission to spread the word of Yahweh's love to all the nations. So in the end, Yahweh forced them out, scattering them across the nations. And in some strange, shocking and curiously beautiful way, the Israelite's punishment for disobedience - a punishment of last resorts (Lev. 26:27) - has actually led to hearts from many nationalities ditching their idols and falling in love with Yahweh.

Astonishing.

Destruction and exile have actually advanced the ambitions of Phase Four.

From death has come life.

Feeling compelled to pray, Nehemiah steps back from the euphoric celebrations spiralling around the Temple courtyard. 'Thank you Yahweh,' Nehemiah begins, his volume masked by the music and laughter. 'Thank you for your *good plans for* us; plans to give us *hope and a good future* (Jer. 29:11).'

Nehemiah pauses. He gulps.

'But you had good plans for us before Yahweh, and look what happened to us. We were like clay in your hands, Jeremiah said. You were shaping us, moulding us, *but something went wrong* (Jer. 18:4). We did not want to be moulded. We rejected your plans and spun away on our own accord, ending up in a horrible mess.

'Oh Yahweh, this time, we choose to stay in your hands. This time, craft us into the stunning piece of art, shape us into the decoration of your love, the way you originally intended us to be (Jer. 18:4).'

Before Nehemiah realises what is happening he has been swept away by the dance swinging its way around the Temple courtyard. *The sound of happiness in Jerusalem* is *heard far away* (Neh. 12:43) as the whole city sings:

'*Praise God in his Temple;*
  Praise him in his mighty heaven.
Praise him for his strength;
  Praise him for his greatness…
Praise him with tambourines and dancing…
Let everything that breathes praise Yahweh (Ps. 150:2-6).'

'*When* Yahweh *brought the prisoners back to Jerusalem,*
  It seemed as if we were dreaming.
Then we were filled with laughter,
  And we sang happy songs.
Then the nations said,
  "Yahweh *has done great things for them* (Ps.126:1-2)."'

'*Shout and rejoice together,*
  Because Yahweh *has comforted his people.*
He has saved Jerusalem.
Yahweh *will show his holy power*
  To all the nations.
Then everyone on earth
  Will see the salvation of our God (Is. 52:9-10).'

PHASE FIVE

5.01 - Blasphemy

Tears tumble chaotically from Abba's distressed and torn, passionate and longing eyes. Wracked with grief, Abba's mournful gaze is fixed upon the excruciating plight of one man clothed only in blood, clinging helplessly to his final moments of life. This precious child of Abba, this masterpiece of Elohim, hangs humiliated from two rugged wooden beams, arms swept out across the horizontal, legs draped down the vertical. Completely exhausted, drained of all energy, for one final time the man screams out. Then he is gone, breathing no more.

At the moment of loss, Abba too cries out, audibly letting loose his distress. This man now hanging limp, absent of life, was loved beyond measure. And the greatest tragedy of all is that the man never even knew it. This dearly desired, delicately crafted life fell so short of his stunning potential. All beauty was hijacked from within him. Enticed by revenge, this man robbed others of life. And for murder he has paid the ultimate price. His execution was the most bloody and gruesome demise ever devised by human hand.

Struck still by her heartbreak, Ruach hovers motionless above a valley between two hilltops. On one side is the execution site. On the other, Jerusalem, the city which Ruach once called home; the city from which a kingdom of peace and life, justice, freedom and equality - a kingdom of heaven - once spread out through the surrounding nations.

Today, fear fills Jerusalem. Nehemiah's reforms of four hundred years ago are now nothing more than a fleeting, distant, tantalising memory. All in Jerusalem must bow to the most powerful dominion of all: the Roman Empire.

All must declare 'Caesar is Lord.'

And acknowledge Herod as their King.

Or face the ultimate retribution: crucifixion.

Each drip of blood from a crucified rebel communicates a chilling political message: put a foot out of line, dare to disrupt the peace, dare to challenge the Empire's authority, and this is how you shall spend your final hours.

You shall die as a disgraced public spectacle.

You shall die as an outcast, tied to a disfigured tree outside the city walls.

The excruciating prospect haunts the Jews in Jerusalem more than most: according to their ancient laws, '*anyone who is hung on a tree is under God's curse (Deut. 21:23).*'

Our fist thumps the Phase Five wall in petulant frustration.

'How long must this curse go on?' we scream helplessly.

'Where are you, Yahweh?

'Why are you so silent?

'What has happened to Rescue?

'What has happened to your love?'

Our jarring words hang in the silence, tangled in tight choked air. Our chest contracts, as if battling an acute hunger.

'*People will wander through the land troubled and hungry (Is. 8:21).*'

The silence broken, our back clicks rigid.

'*They will look up and curse their king and their God. They will look around them at their land and see only trouble, darkness and awful gloom (Is. 8:21-22).*'

Though we have no sense of where it comes from, this voice sounds real and honest. It seems to connect with our pain. Stirred by concern, it soothes us.

'*But suddenly there will be no more gloom for the land that suffered (Is. 9:1).*'

As if pulled by the rising tones of optimism even the air seems to loosen and our eyes focus once more on the Headquarters wall. To our great surprise the next words we read are those just heard.

And elaboration follows:

'*A child has been born to us; God has given a son to us.*

He will be responsible for leading the people.

His name will be Wonderful Counsellor,

Powerful God,

Father Who Lives For Ever,

Prince of Peace.

Power and peace will be in his kingdom…

He will rule as king on David's throne (Is. 9:6-7).'

Scepticism explodes within us: some of these credentials are just futile nonsense.

How could a father live forever?!

Worse still, how could a human be 'Powerful God'?!

Isn't this the most outrageous blasphemy?

A scribbled footnote tells us that this text was first uttered by Isaiah over seven centuries before Jerusalem's Roman occupation. Dismissing Isaiah as insane, with a stroppy child-like swing of the arm we rip the passage down from the wall.

Beneath it lays further narrative.

In an impoverished impromptu shelter, with a waft of farmyard faeces filling the air, a young teenage mother rests in the arms of her fiancé. Exhausted but elated, overwhelmed by love, Mary sits captivated by the tiny rhythmic breaths of her new born son.

So beautiful and tender.

So precious and fragile.

So helpless and innocent.

Could it really be true? Could this miniature bundle of joy asleep in her arms really be Israel's long-awaited great warrior?

Israel's Messiah?

Rescuer?

A liberator like Moses?

The one described by Isaiah?

Ruling on the throne of David?

Reigning over a universal kingdom of peace?

The Roman Empire may already claim to be a universal kingdom of peace, but it is peace by coercion, peace by fear. Extortionate taxes keep the rich in power and the poor in poverty. And worse still, in the last few years the Emperor Augustus has even had the audacity to start describing himself as, 'the son of the gods.' Temples are being built all over the Empire to worship Augustus as a god on earth.

A god in human flesh.

For Mary this is the most outrageous blasphemy, the ultimate denial of Yahweh. This is the ultimate oppression, the utmost reason why the tiny child asleep in Mary's arms simply has to fulfil his liberation mission, and *rule over the people of Jacob forever* (Luke 1:33).

Forever.

Forever.

Because *nothing is impossible with God* (Luke 1:37).

Nothing.

Is impossible.

Mary knows it is true.

Because nine months ago, Mary experienced the impossible first hand.

Despite being a virgin, despite having never had sex, Mary fell pregnant.

And a virgin becoming pregnant is a much anticipated, highly significant sign. Isaiah wrote about a young mother naming her miracle child *'Immanuel* (Isaiah 7:14),' meaning 'God with us.' The child would be the sign that God's favour had returned. The curse would be over. God would be for us, with us, once again.

Mary leans down and kisses her Immanuel's forehead, overwhelmed by the knowledge that she is the most privileged woman of all time. Her miraculous conception was caused by the life-bringing breath of Ruach.

Which means, the child in her arms, truly, literally is 'God with us.'

The child she kisses, truly, literally is '*the Son of God* (Luke 1:35).'

Mary is holding Yahweh in human flesh.

5.02 - Jesus the Great

Four hundred years ago in Babylon the Messiah arrived.

The Messiah liberated the exiles.

Or so they thought.

Cyrus the Great, the King of Persia, swept in from the east, winning battle after battle, and he was hailed as Yahweh's *appointed king.* *'He is my shepherd,'* Yahweh said of Cyrus. *'He will say to Jerusalem, "You will be built again!* (Is. 44:28)'"

And he did.

Cyrus set the exiles free.

His policies of tolerance were so unprecedented, and his timing so accurately fulfilled Jeremiah's seventy years of exile prophecy (Jer. 29:10), that the returning exiles became convinced: Yahweh had surely sent Cyrus to save them.

But as the years passed, doubts rose over Cyrus' Messiah credentials. The prophet Ezekiel had seen a vision of the exiles returning to a paradise, a paradise like that promised to Abraham and Moses. But in reality, the exiles returned to a barren and derelict Jerusalem, still ravaged by its Babylonian destruction.

So perhaps Zerubbabel had been the true Messiah? He'd rebuilt Jerusalem's Temple and a Temple was at the heart of Ezekiel's paradise vision. What's more, Zerubbabel was a direct descendant of David, the rightful heir to Judah's throne.

Or perhaps the Messiah was Nehemiah? He'd administered justice, freedom and equality: all prominent features in Ezekiel's paradise (Ez. 45:9-10).

But then Alexander the Great started overthrowing Persian power wherever he led his army, and before long, the Judeans were wondering whether Alexander would be their Messiah? The Judeans surrendered willingly to Alexander's revolution and sure enough, the prolific killer spared their blood. Even Egypt welcomed Alexander as their great liberator, honouring him as Pharaoh, revering him as a son of the gods.

A god in human flesh.

Alexander was revered for ushering in a whole new world.

A Greek world.

A world more enlightened and developed.

A world built upon the teachings of Pythagoras, Plato and Aristotle.

But the new world brought with it difficulties, particularly for the Jews trying to live in careful adherence to Yahweh's laws. An athletics stadium built in Jerusalem not only forced participants to compete naked - embarrassing enough for circumcised Jews - but each sporting spectacle was dedicated to Zeus, King of the Greek gods.

Uncomfortable cultural compromises continued.

Until Judah's Greek King made the situation untenable.

King Antiochus chose to outlaw all practices honouring Yahweh.

And enforced the worship of Zeus.

Antiochus even declared himself as the visible manifestation of Zeus.

A god in human flesh.

Failure to submit was punishable by death.

Now more than ever the Judeans needed their Messiah, their own 'Great' warrior like Cyrus or Alexander.

Step forward Judas Maccabeus.

With a poorly equipped band of amateurs, Judas Maccabeus tore into Antiochus' army. He destroyed all traces of Zeus and liberated Jerusalem from Greek rule. Over the next eighty years the politically independent Maccabean dynasty stretched out its borders and Ezekiel's vision of a restored Israel (Ez. 48:1-8), as large as that ruled by King David, edged ever closer.

Judas Maccabeus was the Messiah.

Wasn't he?

'*I will live here among the Israelites forever* (Ez.43:7),' Yahweh cheered in Ezekiel's vision of paradise. 'The city will be known as, "Yahweh *Is There* (Ez. 48:35)."'

Yet when Roman General Pompey stormed into Jerusalem, claiming it for the new world superpower he marched straight into the Temple's Holy of Holies and revealed a truly shocking secret. Inside the exclusive room famously housing the awesome Shekinah of Yahweh, Pompey found nothing.

He saw no swirling cloud.

He felt no tangible presence.

Because the devastating truth was: Yahweh was not there. Ever since Jerusalem's demolition, the Shekinah had never returned to dwell in her Temple.

Ezekiel's paradise had clearly not arrived yet.

Ezekiel's vision also contained a river.

A river teaming with life.

A river filled with everlasting water.

Living water.

Water bringing the dead to life (Ez. 47:9).

Water nurturing leaves that never *dry and die.*

Leaves which heal the city's inhabitants like *medicine* (Ez. 47:12).

Ezekiel's paradise had clearly not arrived yet.

Confused and bewildered, the Jewish scholars started to pour over the prophecies from their past, desperate to fathom out what was going on. They discovered that Daniel had added to Jeremiah's seventy years of exile by describing a further period of four hundred and ninety years before '*the appointed leader comes* (Dan. 9:25).' During that time, Daniel had foreseen the rise and fall of three further kingdoms (Dan. 2:39-40) before one final kingdom, the Kingdom of God, 'crushed *all the other kingdoms* and continued *forever* (Dan. 2:44).'

So far, history has proved Daniel right.

First Cyrus the Great inaugurated the Persian Kingdom.

Then Alexander the Great brought the world of the Greeks.

And now Herod the Great rules within the Empire of Rome.

But Daniel's four hundred and ninety years are nearly up. Very soon it will be time for Ezekiel's paradise, the Kingdom of God, to arrive.

King Herod is on full alert. In order to cling onto his power, Herod is trying his hardest to present himself as the Judean's Messiah. He calls himself 'The King of the Jews,' and is putting considerable effort into reconstructing Jerusalem's Temple. Having slain challenger after challenger to earn the powerful position he enjoys, Herod is anxious to eliminate the true Messiah before it is too late.

So when Herod hears news that the Messiah may have been born in Bethlehem, he does not hesitate before striking. Herod orders the death of all *baby boys in Bethlehem* (Matt. 2:16).

Thirty years later, Jesus is sitting by a well, desperate for a drink, sweltering in the midday sun, when a woman approaches to draw water.

'*Whoever drinks the water I give will never be thirsty again,*' Jesus says to the woman. '*The water I give will become a spring of water flowing up inside that person, giving eternal life* (John 4:13).'

Taken aback, the woman pauses, not knowing how to reply. By referencing Ezekiel's living, everlasting water, this arrogant stranger has touched upon her nation's deepest aches and pains, longings and expectations; a topic clouded with confusion and rumour, claims and counter-claims.

'*I know that the Messiah is coming,*' the woman replies. '*When the Messiah comes he will explain everything* (John 4:25).'

Jesus looks the woman in the eye; and with the smile of someone revealing a long kept secret, says, '*I am he - I, the one talking to you* (John 4:26).'

Ezekiel's paradise has arrived.

The kingdom of God is now.

For the revolution of Jesus the Great is about to begin.

5.03 - The Pivotal Moment

A grin flickers across our face; our eyes alight in wonder. The words of Ezekiel's vision have reached down through the centuries and seeped into the consciousness of Jesus' world. But more incredible than that, here beneath our feet, buried amongst the debris of our fall from the loft, there are potentially hundreds of similar Phase Four texts.

Each could shape our understanding of Phase Five.

Each could reveal Jesus' motivations and ambitions.

Each could illuminate his actions and achievements.

So with renewed vigour we fall down to our knees and start to sieve through the Phase Four wreckage. Occasionally, to our delight, we uncover an entire scroll which has survived the fall without much damage. But more often than not we only recover tattered fragments, ripped and torn; which will require some considerable work to piece back together.

It's not long before we have made our first connection.

'I became very angry and hid from you for a time, but I will show you mercy with kindness forever.'

Our head shakes in bewilderment as we read the words again. *'This day is like the time of Noah to me. I promised then that I would never flood the world again. In the same way, I promise I will not be angry with you or punish again* (Is. 54:8-9).'

Really? Is there really a day coming when Yahweh's anger and punishments will be no more? Is that not too good to be true?

Our journey so far has taught us that God is Love.

And Love demands justice.

And justice demands punishment.

But the second text in our hand is clear: *'I will make an everlasting covenant with them: I will never stop doing good to them* (Jer. 32:40*).'

This shakes us to the very core of our being.

This shakes our very view of God: it shakes our fear.

'I will enjoy doing good to them. And with my whole being I will surely plant them in this land and make them grow (Jer. 32:41).'

Our heart flutters and skips. There is a day coming when Yahweh's goodness will be everlasting; covenanted, contracted, for all time.

Somehow - and we have no idea how - there is a moment coming, a pivotal moment, when the God of Love and Justice ceases to dispense punishments. And from that moment onwards only goodness will remain.

We spring back to our feet. Perhaps Jesus is going to bring about this moment?

Right from a young age Jesus has stood out as a prodigy of the texts. At only twelve years old his wisdom and insights into the records and writings of Israel's ancestors have impressed even the most knowledgeable scholars of Jerusalem.

And in today's Jewish world, that elevates Jesus to an extremely important and responsible position in society. As the Babylonian exile proved, a correct interpretation and faithful application of these ancient texts really does hold the key to choosing life over death.

Every week, the local communities gather in their synagogues to be reminded of the importance of following Yahweh's Laws. And in recent months, Jesus has been out on the road, sharing his insights in synagogue after synagogue.

Today, the prodigy has returned home. Today, Jesus shall teach his family and friends in the synagogue he grew up in, the synagogue which educated him.

The congregation is far from silent as Jesus stands up from his seat and the book of Isaiah is handed to him. 'Do you remember when...' friends whisper to each other, recalling fond memories from Jesus' childhood.

Jesus looks up. He is ready. There's a twinkle in his eye. He has found his page. '*The Lord has put his Spirit in me, because he appointed me to tell the Good News to the poor. He has sent me to tell the captives they are free and to tell the blind that they can see again* (Luke 4:18).'

We instantly recognise the words. These were the first words on the scroll we found, the one that survived our Phase Four fall. We unravel the scroll with care-filled reverence. The scroll is filled with stanza after stanza of romantic poetry:

'*Because I love Jerusalem,*' one portion begins.

 '*You will never again be called the People that God Left,*
Nor your land the land that God Destroyed.
 You will be called the People God Loves,

126

And your land will be called the Bride of God...
As a man rejoices over his new wife,
  So your God will rejoice over you (Is. 62:1-5).'

Once again the language is absolute: Jerusalem will never ever again be destroyed. Yahweh's punishments will be no more. It is finished. Only Yahweh's goodness, Yahweh's tender restoration, only Yahweh's love and celebration will remain.

This is the pivotal moment described again.

As we read onwards, the Rescue Mission's long-term aspirations expand further. They stretch far beyond the restoration of one city and reach a scale of universal proportions.

'*Look, I will make new heavens and a new earth* (Is. 65:17).' Yahweh says in the scroll. And on this new earth, '*a person who lives one hundred years will be called young* (Is. 65:20).'

On this new earth, there will be no more crying.

No more pain.

No more injustice.

No more bloodshed.

Not even animals will kill each other (Is. 65:17-18).

'*Like babies you will be nursed and held in my arms and bounced on my knees,*' the tender romantic Yahweh promises. '*I will comfort you as a mother comforts her child* (Is. 66:12-13).'

This will be the age of everlasting kindness.

This is the age that every Jew is waiting for, hoping for, longing for.

And this is the text that Jesus has chosen to read in the synagogue.

'*God sent me,*' Jesus continues, '*to free those who have been treated unfairly, and to announce the time when the Lord will show his kindness* (Luke 4:19).'

Absolute silence.

All are struck still by a thought of cataclysmic proportions.

When Jesus just said, 'God sent me,' was he saying...? Was he... is he saying that the time of the Lord's kindness is... is actually here? Now?

A smile stretches out across Jesus' cheeks.

'*While you heard these words just now,*' his words build to a momentous crescendo: '*they were coming true! (Luke 4:21)*'

The pivotal moment has arrived.

5.04 - A New Israel

His flesh shrivelled like rotting fruit, Jesus staggers and falls and collapses into a field of gorgeous green grass. For forty days Jesus has been living in the wilderness, living where no-one can live, out in the blistering desert. With nothing to eat or drink Jesus has pushed his body to its limits, exposing himself to mental agony and torment.

And as we imagine Jesus recovering, lying out on the grass, stretching his tongue to lick rain drops from a leaf, we wonder why?

Why would Jesus put himself through all that?

To mentally prepare himself for the challenges ahead?

To test and train his body for combat?

Or was it a symbolic act, to send out a message to the masses?

The forty days was not an arbitrary number. Forty is a number of great significance, not least because Israel had to wait forty years in the desert before entering the Promised Land.

Dots start to join in our mind.

As we look back over the beginnings of Phase Five, we notice further connections between Jesus' life and the history of Israel. For starters, Jesus was born in Bethlehem, the home of. David. Then King Herod ordered the massacre of all baby boys in Bethlehem, just like the Egyptian Pharaoh at the beginning of Phase Three. Moses' mother saved her babe from the Pharaoh's butchery, and likewise Jesus' parents fled with their precious child to Egypt.

Where they stayed until Herod died.

Which means, Jesus came out of Egypt (Matt. 2:15).

Just like Israel.

Then there's the list of Jesus' twelve closest supporters, the men who form the central hub of Jesus' growing army. Jesus has chosen twelve men in his inner circle to deliberately echo the twelve tribes of Israel, hasn't he?

The evidence appears compelling: whether consciously or sub-consciously, Jesus' life so far is retelling Israel's story.

But to what extent, we wonder?

Will Jesus continue to re-enact the story exactly as it happened, warts and all?

Will his life include a Babylonian exile?

Or will Jesus tell the story how it was supposed to happen?

Will Jesus 'choose life'?

Suddenly a voice stuns us still.

'*Your mother was like a vine… the vine had many branches and gave much fruit.*'

The voice is not from above or below us, behind or in front. It just seems to surround us; cut right through us.

'*But* the vine *was pulled up by its roots in anger and thrown to the ground (Ez. 19:10-12). I planted you as a special vine, as a very good seed. How then did you turn into a wild vine that grows bad fruit? (Jer. 2:21)*'

The voice is more than just exasperated. It's devastated; totally distraught, as if grieving the loss of a loved one.

'*What more could I have done for my vineyard? … Although I expected good grapes to grow, why were there only bad ones? (Is. 5:4)*'

The voice chokes as if tears have dripped into the mourner's mouth.

'*This is a funeral song; it is to be used as a funeral song (Ez. 19:14).*'

We feel moved by the words, moved by the emotion, but we do not know why. We do not understand why anyone would be singing a funeral song over the loss of some grapes. Who is the vine?

Our eyes sweep over the Phase Five wall, searching for references to grapes or vines. Sure enough, up in the top right-hand corner, in letters so large we cannot miss them, Jesus says, '*I am the true vine (John 15:1).*'

But hang on, if Jesus is the vine, does this mean that Jesus went sour?

Is Jesus the one that the voice is mourning?

That can't be right.

Thankfully the quote is written onto card only attached to the wall along one folded hinge. Written underneath the makeshift flap, Isaiah explains, '*The vineyard belonging to* Yahweh *is the nation of Israel; the garden that he loves is the people of Judah. He looked for justice, but there was only killing. He hoped for right living, but there were only cries of pain (Is. 5:7).*'

So Israel was the vine that went sour, not Jesus. Now it makes sense. So when Jesus describes himself as 'the true vine' he is identifying himself as a new Israel, a true Israel, the embodiment of everything that

Israel was originally meant to be. He will be the justice that Yahweh has always sought, the right living that was craved.

To the left of the vine revelation, another hinged card catches our attention. In a vivid royal blue font, Jesus says, '*I am the good shepherd* (John 10:11).'

What does he mean this time?

Without a second thought we lift the flap and peer beneath. Immediately a line highlighted in yellow stands out: '*This is what the Lord GOD says: I myself, will search for my sheep and take care of them* (Ez. 34:11).'

In this text Ezekiel describes how Israel was let down by a catalogue of incompetent, self-indulgent leaders. '*The sheep were scattered, because there was no shepherd, and they became food for every wild animal* (Ez. 34:5-6).'

Then the highlighted line signals a shift in the account. Ezekiel begins to describe how Yahweh will round up his scattered sheep. Yahweh will be Israel's one true, good shepherd and will lead his flock home to abundant idyllic pastures. '*I will make a covenant of peace with them,*' says shepherd Yahweh, '*and rid the land of wild beasts* (Ez. 34:25*).'

The lost sheep have been rounded up.

They have been brought home from the nations.

And now Jesus says, 'I am the good shepherd.'

Jesus is poised to initiate paradise and establish Yahweh's covenant of peace. But to attain paradise and peace, Jesus must first rid Jerusalem of its wild beasts.

Jesus must destroy the imperious Romans.

5.05 - Invincible

Peter knows how it works by now. All James has to do is throw out some brash, absolute statement and his younger brother John takes the bait. No matter how obvious it is that John is right, James never backs down; he just enjoys winding his brother up too much.

At the best of times the immature tussles test Peter's patience.

But today...

Today Peter is sitting on a jagged rock high up a mountain, it is cold and overcast, and he is completely alone with the two brothers. If Jesus wasn't off praying in the distance, Peter would have wrung their necks long ago.

'We should never have abandoned our father's business. At least fishing gave us a secure future.' James flings his arm out in the direction of Jesus. 'This madman could get us killed.'

'We made our decision and we stick to it. No-one would turn down a chance to follow a rabbi like this.'

'But is he even a rabbi, John? No true rabbi would have ever taken us as disciples. Not after we dropped out of the synagogue education at such a young age. We've been taken in by a rogue, a showman, a wannabe. I mean, what rabbi ever calls God, "Abba"? They don't even call God...' James lowers his voice, '"Yahweh" anymore.'

John shoots his brother a disapproving glare. 'James, you've seen what he's done. I've lost count of the number of people he's healed. And you know that he uses no tricks. This man is like Moses or Elijah. They both spoke intimately with God up Mount Sinai (1 Kings 19:13) and that's what Jesus is doing now. He calls God, "Abba" because they have a close relationship.'

'It's all part of the act, John; just another of his outrageous claims. You heard Jesus when he said, "Moses wrote about me (John 5:46)." How could Moses have possibly written about Jesus? Then he said that he had come to fulfil all of Moses' laws (Matt. 5:17). That's ridiculous, impossible. This man is just arrogant, obnoxious, out of his mind.'

'No, James. You're the one who's obnoxious. Jesus is the most intelligent man you've ever met. He summed up Moses' entire law, every clause and sub-clause, in just one sentence: *"Do to others what you want them to do to you (Matt. 7:12)."* Only a truly exceptional man could have managed such a feat. His teaching emphasised our motives, our attitudes, our thoughts, our heart (Matt. 5:21-48). And when he was teaching the crowds on that mountain, you've got to admit that he looked a bit like Moses.'

'But on another day he said that he was *"greater than Solomon (Matt. 12:42);"* then he claimed he was *"greater than the Temple (Matt. 12:6)."* That's not intelligent, that's just deranged! The Temple housed God's Shekinah. No-one could...'

In one swift motion, Peter is bearing down on James, pressing his finger into James' cheek and up into his eye. Through gritted teeth he yells, 'He is the Messiah (Matt. 16:16), you idiot! Why can't you see that? *Even the winds and waves obey him!* (Mark 4:41) We were going to die in that storm and all Jesus said was, *"Quiet! Be still!"* (Mark 4:39) and the waves cowered in retreat. He made me walk on water. He is *the Son of God* (Matt. 14:33).'

James dare not speak.

'Lay off him Peter. You can't know for sure that Jesus is the Messiah.'

Peter looks round, eyes blazing, staggered by John's defence of his brother.

'Having power over sea doesn't make Jesus the Messiah. It just makes him like Moses; or like Elijah and Elisha, who both parted the Jordan River (2 Kings 2:8, 2 Kings 2:13).'

Peter pulls back his finger from James' eye. His shoulders slump in exasperation. 'But Jesus is better than Moses, Elijah and Elisha. Elisha fed one hundred people with twenty loaves and a sack of grain, and there was *food left over* (2 Kings 4:44). Well, Jesus fed thousands of people with just five loaves and two fish, and we *filled twelve baskets with* the leftovers (Matt. 14:20).

'What's more, Elijah and Elisha both revived one dead child (1 Kings 17:22, 2 Kings 4:37). But Jesus has already revived two dead children (Luke 7:14, Luke 8:54). And who's to say he won't do it again.'

'That still doesn't make him the Messiah; just a really great prophet (Luke 7:16).'

'But you seem to have forgotten that Elijah was *taken up to heaven in a whirlwind* (2 Kings 2:11). Elijah never died. So if Jesus is better than

Elijah then Jesus won't die either. Jesus will be totally unstoppable when he takes on the Romans. He'll be invincible.'

'But Peter, Jesus can't be the Messiah because *Elijah must come first* (Matt. 17:10). Malachi said that Elijah would return before the *"great and terrible day of the LORD's judging"* (Mal. 4:5), before the Romans *"burn like a hot furnace* (Mal. 4:1)."'

A blazing fireball explodes.

Through shielded eyes, the three peer out to see Jesus' *face* shining *bright like the sun, his clothes* a vehement *white* (Matt. 17:2). Two mysterious men stand beside Jesus, talking to him. Then a voice booms across the sky, '*This is my Son, whom I love, and I am very pleased with him* (Matt. 17:5).'

Peter, James and John fall flat to the ground.

They do not know how long it is until an arm ushers them up.

'You're ok. You're ok.'

Jesus' smile is warm.

The lights have gone; so too have his companions.

Jesus helps Peter, James and John to their feet and as they start to walk down the mountain Jesus reveals that he has just been having a conversation with Moses and Elijah.

And for the next hour John does not hear another word Jesus says.

Because Elijah!

Elijah!

Elijah has returned.

The day of judgment is imminent.

The day when justice is done.

The day when the first become last and the last become first (Matt. 19:30).

When *the proud and evil* become *like straw* (Mal. 4:1).

On this coming judgment day, not even the mighty Romans will be able to withstand Jesus' invincible onslaught. The blood that Jesus spills will liberate the world.

5.06 - Life to the Dead

It is nearly ten years since the smooth golden oil poured over Caiaphas' head and raced down his robes. Anointed as high priest of Jerusalem, appointed with Rome's full approval, on that day Caiaphas had felt ready for anything. All he had to do was keep the peace in Jerusalem and Rome's blessing was assured.

Caiaphas sighs. Down every Jerusalem street, swords are being sharpened. Thanks to Jesus the whole of Jerusalem believes that revolution is imminent. Leaving Caiaphas with a colossal decision to make: either he follows the populous and throws his weight behind this man who has apparently revived a man who had been dead for four days? Or he stops Jesus before it is too late?

To help him make up his mind, Caiaphas has called an emergency meeting, a gathering of Jerusalem's most eminent religious leaders.

'If Jesus continues to do these things, *everyone will believe in him. The Romans will come and take away our Temple and our nation* (John 11:48).'

Caiaphas sits forlorn as advice flies at him from every angle.

'Jesus will ignite the wrath of Rome. Their retaliation could wipe out Israel in a day; God's chosen people would be gone forever.'

'We gave Jesus his chance. We asked him straight out, "*If you are the Christ tell us plainly* (John 10:24)." The true Messiah would never hide his identity. But do you know what Jesus said? "*The father and I are one* (John 10:30)"! What kind of answer is that?'

'He's pretty much saying that he is God. Who ever said that the Messiah would be our LORD? Everyone knows that a god in human flesh is no god at all. This Jesus just doesn't know what he is talking about. Tell me, where did he study?'

'He says that his teaching "*comes from God* (John 17:7)." He said, and I quote, "*I was sent by the One who is true… I am from him, and he sent me* (John 7:28-29)."'

'It's just sheer arrogance.'

'It's lunacy.'

'It's blasphemy! *Anyone who blasphemes the name of the LORD must be put to death* (Lev. 24:16*).'

'Jesus' lies are dangerous. He just says what people want to hear. Jesus even claimed, "*whoever obeys my teaching will never die* (John 8:51)."'

'Thankfully the crowds didn't just swallow that one. "*Even Abraham and the prophets died,*" they shouted out, "*Do you think that you are greater than our father Abraham?* (John 8:53-54)"'

'You won't believe what Jesus said in reply. He said, "*Abraham was very happy that he would see my day* (John 8:56).'"

The usually civil council erupts in derision.

Caiaphas signals for quiet.

'Who can testify that Jesus said this?'

More than half the room raises their hand.

'But sir, there is more. When the crowds shouted, "*You have never seen Abraham! You are not even 50 years old*" Jesus' response was so abhorrent, well, I can't even repeat it.'

'You have to. I have to know.'

'You won't like it. He said: "*I tell you the truth, before Abraham was even born, I am!* (John 8:57-58)"'

Caiaphas bows his head.

He has heard enough.

Jesus must die.

Our hands trace through our hair and slide down over our face as the true horror of the situation sinks in. Jesus is telling the truth and yet we cannot blame the priests for reacting as they have. By saying, 'Before Abraham was born I am,' Jesus is implying that he is thousands of years old. Who would honestly believe that?

The phrase rocks about in our mind.

'Before Abraham... I am': it's such a curious phrase. Why would Jesus say it like that? Why not say, 'I was alive before Abraham'? Why 'I am'?

'I am.

'I am.

'I am that I am.'

We click our fingers as we realise it. 'I am' is a direct reference to the name 'Yahweh.' Jesus said 'I am' to deliberately connect himself with Yahweh.

Our muscles relax.

Back in Phase Three, Moses' Egyptian liberation had seemed impossible.

But with Yahweh it was possible.

And Jesus' is Yahweh in human flesh.

His victory is guaranteed.

Because Jesus is all-powerful.

Invincible.

Jesus cannot die.

Mary feels her heart beat as she looks into Jesus' eyes and strokes his rugged hair. This is the greatest man she will ever know. He is kind and compassionate, honest and raw. When her brother Lazarus died, Mary saw the extent of Jesus' heartbreak, she saw the tears streaming down his face (John 11:35).

Mary looks across at Lazarus laughing, sharing a joke with Jesus' disciples. The precious sight leaves Mary in no doubt: Jesus has to be the Messiah. He has brought life to the dead. He is '*the resurrection and the life* (John 11:25).'

Mary has seen the new creation breaking out before her very eyes. Resurrection is possible. And it is here, now. These are the last days of the old world, the final days before Yahweh's ultimate rescue, where Yahweh brings life to the dead (John 11:24).

And Lazarus has already risen: Jesus has to be the Messiah.

Yet Mary looks into Jesus' eyes.

And she cannot help but fear for his life.

This man that she loves so dearly: he is no great warrior.

He is strong and confident, brave and assured. But he is no fighter.

Jesus lacks a warrior spirit.

King David was Israel's greatest warrior, winning battle after battle, expanding Israel's borders, liberating from enemies all around. But David never fought in his own strength. It was the anointing breath of Ruach who gave David his success. When he was just a boy, smooth golden oil was poured over his head and *from that day on, the LORD's Spirit worked in David* (1 Sam. 16:13).

Jesus needs dousing in the same warrior spirit King David had.

For 'Messiah' literally means 'the anointed one.'

Mary lifts up a bottle of her finest perfume and pours the rich aromatic oil over Jesus' head. The crowded room falls unerringly silent.

Jesus closes his eyes as the liquid flows over his body and down to his feet. Next Mary loosens her hair down to her waist and wipes back and forth, massaging and drying Jesus' feet.

Shock turns to outrage.

Frantic protests fly.

Aware of the commotion, Jesus wipes the oil from his eyes. He looks around the room, catching every eye; then announces, '*It was right for Mary to save this perfume for today, the day for me to be prepared for burial* (John 12:7).'

5.07 - How The Tables Have Turned

Judas Iscariot lies on his back, staring out at the stars, marvelling at the world in which he lives. When dawn breaks, he will be fighting in the war to end all wars, fighting for the new Jerusalem promised by the prophets; a Jerusalem free from oppression and injustice, overflowing with peace and prosperity; a Jerusalem that the God of Abraham will be proud to call home.

With one hand permanently fixed to the hilt of his sword, Judas mentally rehearses each swing of his weapon. Picking out a light in the sky, he tries to focus his mind.

'It was right for Mary to save this perfume for today, the day for me to be prepared for burial (John 12:7).'

Judas screws up his eyes: just when he is fully focussed on the battle ahead, these words of Jesus come back and haunt him. What did Jesus mean? Was he conceding defeat?! Is Jesus expecting to die in this war?!

Judas shakes his head, physically throwing the thought from his mind. In its place, another terrifying image takes over: the sight of Jesus, only yesterday, breaking down in a flood of tears.

Why, Jesus, why?

This was a humiliating public display of weakness.

This was not Messiah.

As Jesus wept he explained his tears. *'You did not recognise the time when God came to save you (Luke 19:44),'* Jesus exclaimed in exasperation. But Judas cannot understand it; the vast majority had recognised the time when God came to save them. It was only the religious leaders who had wanted to shut down Jesus' triumphal entry into Jerusalem. Which was hardly surprising since they are puppets to Rome; the system works for them.

Forget the religious leaders, Judas pleads to the night. We have all the support we need.

When Jesus rode toward Jerusalem, awkwardly and ungainly on that young donkey, everyone knew what Jesus was saying. Everyone recognised his deliberate enactment of Zechariah's well-known Messianic prophecy:

'Rejoice greatly, people of Jerusalem!
Shout for joy, people of Jerusalem!
Your king is coming for you.
He does what is right, and he saves.
He is gentle and riding on a donkey,
On the colt of a donkey (Zech. 9:9).'

What's more, the timing of Jesus' announcement was impeccable. With this year's Passover celebrations just days away, what better time to announce the new rescue of the Israelites than at the annual commemoration of Moses' remarkable rescue!

Jerusalem is awash with pilgrims in the city for the festivities. And the cosmopolitan crowd cheered Jesus at the top of their voice: '*God bless the kingdom of our father David! That kingdom is coming!* (Mark 11:10)'

Judas grins. Slowly he slides his hand down his blade and leaves his finger resting on its tip. When dawn breaks, Judas will fight for Jesus' revolution.

And he will fight for his life.

With fire in his eyes Jesus strides menacingly, looking every bit a warrior. Eyes fixed firmly upon his target, he storms into the Temple courtyard and crashes into the commercial traders, turning over their tables, sending their merchandise sprawling. '*My Temple will be called a house of prayer,*' Jesus roars. '*But you are changing it into a 'hideout for robbers'* (Matt. 21:13).'

For Jesus' opening strike he has targeted Rome's commercial corruption of Jerusalem's most sacred venue. The Temple worshippers were a captive market, enabling the merchants to charge extortionate prices for substandard products.

With the merchants scarpering, next Jesus ushers in those previously prohibited from the courtyard. Into the merchants' place, he welcomes in society's outcasts. And for the rest of the day Jesus restores sight to the blind and strength to the crippled (Matt. 21:14).

Judas allows himself a smile. Now this is Messiah: fierce and uncompromising, restoring David's Temple, confronting corruption, fighting injustice, bringing dignity, equality, new life and health.

Young children dance with abandon in the courtyard, chanting over and over, 'Praise to the son of David. *Praise to the son of David* (Matt. 21:15).'

This is Messiah: and even energetic kids can see it.

The following day Jesus heads straight to the Temple and starts to teach inside. At first Judas interprets this as one final rallying cry, one final attempt to get the religious leaders on side. But as the day wears on, to Judas' horror, Jesus becomes locked in furious theological debate.

Jesus ducks and dives, avoiding theological traps.

He debates the payment of taxes.

He defends the resurrection of the dead.

He discusses the greatest commandment.

But all the time Jesus is on the defensive, and gaining precious little ground. Judas' patience is waning. Why can't Jesus see that these fiery debates could go on for weeks? Can't Jesus see that he is missing his moment, wasting the wave of optimism and support?

By evening time, there is still no breakthrough. And Jesus too seems to have reached the end of his tether. The fire has returned to his eyes and in a cloud of fury Jesus exits the Temple, turns towards the majestically decorated architecture and yells, '*Do you see all these great buildings? Not one stone will be left on another. Every stone will be thrown to the ground (Mark 13:2).*'

Jesus' followers stand stunned. Only Peter, James, John and Andrew dare follow as their master marches off with a face like thunder.

When the four return a few hours later, they share Jesus' grave expression.

"'*Great trouble will come upon this land,*'" Peter explains, relaying Jesus' words, "'*and God will be angry with these people. They will be killed by the sword and taken as prisoners to all nations. Jerusalem will be crushed (Luke 21:24).*'"

Judas stares out in disbelief at the stars in the night sky.

'Jerusalem will be crushed'!?

'People will be taken as prisoners to all nations'!?

This is not Messiah. This is the opposite of Messiah.

This is judgment, not liberation.

This is Jeremiah, not Moses.

How the tables have turned.

But there's more: next Peter reveals Jesus' prediction that his followers will be hunted down, arrested and killed (Matt. 24:9).

Judas drops his sword to the ground. He fights back the tears starting to well. Judas can see no other way out. There is only one way left for Judas to fight for his life.

Tomorrow, he must go to the high priests and ask, '*What will you pay me for giving Jesus to you? (Matt. 26:15)*'

5.08 - Invitation to Feast

Like Judas, we are also troubled by Jesus' recent comments. Statements such as, 'Jerusalem will be crushed,' cause us to question our most basic understanding of Jesus' mission. Have we completely misunderstood Jesus' intentions?

His mission is to bring about the Kingdom of Heaven on earth, the promised era of God's everlasting kindness. But what if that doesn't mean what we thought it did? What if Jesus is not going to overthrow the Roman Empire?

The next passage of text on the Phase Five wall stands out. It has been circled in thick orange paint; and stretching out from the circle, five arrows point towards annotations of the passage.

The first arrow points to a quotation from Isaiah: 'Yahweh *will prepare a feast on this mountain for all people. It will be a feast with all the best food and wine, the finest meat and wine. On this mountain God will destroy the veil that covers all nations... he will destroy death for ever.* Yahweh *will wipe away every tear from every face. He will take away the shame of his people from the earth* (Is. 25:6-8).'

Destroying death, wiping away every tear, this is the Rescue Mission's ultimate ambition, Love's desired destination. And the triumphal conclusion will be celebrated with a glorious feast.

To which everyone, absolutely everyone, is invited.

'All people.'

'All nations.'

Suddenly it hits us between the eyes: everyone, absolutely everyone, includes Roman soldiers.

Which means... what if, right now, Jesus is seeking to rescue Romans too?

But how... how could Jesus rescue Romans when everyone is expecting him to fight them?

The second arrow tells a story of a Roman general recognising Jesus' power and pleading with the rabbi to heal his bed-stricken servant. Jesus welcomes him. Jesus praises him. Jesus turns to his flabbergasted followers and says, '*This is the greatest faith I have found, even in Israel.*

Many people will come from the east and from the west and will sit and eat with Abraham, Isaac and Jacob in the kingdom of heaven (Matt. 8:11).'

Jesus' words confirm it for us: everyone is invited to the feast in the Kingdom of Heaven. And people from all over the world will chose to attend.

Even Roman soldiers.

'*The kingdom of heaven*,' the third arrow begins, '*is like a king who prepared a wedding feast for his son* (Matt. 22:2). *The king said to his servants… "Go to the street corners and invite everyone you can find to come to my feast* (Matt. 22:8-9).*"*'

The feast in the Kingdom of Heaven will be a romantic wedding banquet.

And everyone is invited.

We look down at the debris beneath our feet as our fall from the Phase Four loft replays in our mind. In Phase Four the Israelites were tasked with sharing their invitation to be the Bride in the most romantic wedding the world will ever know.

But the Israelites rejected their wedding invites (Matt. 22:2-3). They abandoned their mandate to spread the good news. Now Jesus is describing himself as 'the true vine,' the new Israel, the true Israel, the embodiment of everything that Israel was originally meant to be.

Jesus is here to tell the world of Love's great marriage proposal. Yahweh is on earth in human flesh, down on one knee, inviting the world into intimacy.

And those who say 'yes' will sit at Heaven's romantic wedding banquet.

And they shall sit centre of attention.

They shall sit as the newly proclaimed Bride.

The sumptuously beautiful Bride of Love.

The fourth arrow tells us that Jesus was at a wedding when he turned six hundred litres of water into the most sensational wine.

Six hundred litres!

It was Jesus' first miraculous act (John 2:11).

And it was an extravagant visual announcement:

Jesus is here to bring about the Messianic wedding banquet.

So when Jesus turned five loaves into a feast for thousands on a Galilean hillside, the final annotation tells us that this was also a foretaste of the future feast foreseen by Isaiah.

The abundant provisions of both bread and wine were announcements: 'The Kingdom of Heaven is near (Matt. 4:17).'

At last we are ready to read the circled passage.

Jesus has fond childhood memories of the annual Passover festivities in Jerusalem. Every year, his parents would take him to the celebrations of Moses' Egyptian liberation (Luke 2:41).

Every year was a joyous exuberant occasion.

Not this year.

This year, Jesus and his closest followers are secretly locked away in an inconspicuous upstairs room.

Amid high tensions, the room is sombre.

Suspicious.

Wary and apprehensive.

'I wanted very much to eat this Passover meal with you before I suffer,' Jesus explains. 'I will not eat another Passover meal until it is given its true meaning in the kingdom of God (Luke 22:15-16).'

Our jaw drops as we read the words over and over again.

Jesus is going to suffer. And yet the kingdom of God is still coming!?

How? How is that possible?

Next Jesus fills a cup to the brim with wine.

'Take this cup and share it among yourselves (Luke 22:17). When you drink this, do it to remember me (1 Cor. 11:25).'

Jesus takes hold of some bread, breaks it and passes it round the table.

'Eat this in remembrance of me (Luke 22:19*).'

Our confusion persists. Eat this in remembrance of me? Where is Jesus going? Is Jesus - all invincible Jesus - going to be taken away? Arrested? Kidnapped? Held to ransom?

Yet, at the same time, the text seems adamant that Jesus is initiating a whole new Passover feast, a whole new way to revel in his upcoming liberation.

For the future friends and followers of Jesus this is their regular invitation to feast.

The future Bride shall dine on bread and wine.

She shall remember.

Celebrate.

And ache in eager expectation, waiting and longing for the day she marries her one true Love.

Ruach swirls around Abba and, overflowing in perfect love and affection, together they look on, aching in eager expectation, waiting and longing for the day they marry their one true love. Over and over again the Community of Elohim has experienced the heartbreak of rejection. But one day soon their Bride will glide gracefully down the aisle towards them.

It will be the perfect, love drenched wedding.

And Elohim is ready to die for it.

5.09 - There Will Be Blood

Positioned beside the annotated Passover meal narrative, we are intrigued by a page of poetry taped to the wall along its top edge only:

'*I am Israel's father* (Jer. 31:9),' declares Yahweh in a prophecy of Jeremiah.

'*Israel is my dear son,*
  The child that I love.
Yes, I often speak against Israel,
  But I still remember him.
I love him very much
  And I want to comfort him (Jer. 31:20).'

Incredibly, these tender words of affection were spoken in the context of Jerusalem's Babylonian destruction.

'*In the past I watched over Israel and Judah, to pull them up and tear them down, to destroy them and bring them disaster. But now I will watch over them to build them up and make them strong* (Jer. 33:28).'

'*Look, the time is coming,*' declares Yahweh, '*when I will make a new covenant* (Jer. 31:31*).'

New covenant!

New covenant!

The words leap out from the page. Without the covenants so far the Rescue Mission would be nowhere. Each has pulled us closer to the restoration of paradise.

'The new covenant,' says Yahweh, '*will not be like the agreement I made with their ancestors when I took them out of Egypt. I was a husband to them but they broke that agreement* (Jer. 31:32).'

We flinch, recalling the Lover's heartbreak.

'*This is the agreement I will make with the people of Israel… I will forgive them for the wicked things they did, and I will not remember their sins anymore* (Jer. 31:33-34).'

A release of ecstasy rushes up through our body and exits through our mouth like the sound of a slow releasing puncture. This is the pivotal moment again. Yahweh's everlasting era of goodness will be possible because all sins will be forgiven. Punishments will no longer be dispensed because forgiveness will be covenanted, contracted, promised for all time.

But how?

What will happen to make this possible? What will change?

We lift up the Jeremiah page by its top hinge:

'This is my blood,' announces Jesus, holding up a cup filled with wine. *'It is the new covenant that God makes with his people. This blood is poured out for many to forgive their sins (Matt. 26:28).'*

After several minutes of standing and staring, stunned still by the revelation, we eventually stagger back to the centre of the room. We turn round and round, gazing in amazement at the Rescue Mission so far.

Until now the blood of an animal has been offered in place of the punishment that humans deserve. This was forgiveness. This was Love and Justice holding hands.

But now... now there will be a new blood poured out for the forgiveness of sins.

It is promised.

It is covenanted.

There will be blood.

Jesus' blood.

And it is non-negotiable.

It is cold and late, starlight flickers off the greenery, and an arousing perfume of foliage surrounds. Peter nods in gentle appreciation: the olive grove Gethsemane is the perfect atmospheric setting for the drama about to unfold.

'Sit here while I pray (Mark 14:34),' Jesus instructs. Peter hears the nerves in Jesus' voice; the apprehension, the vulnerability, the fear. He sees the beads of sweat sliding over the hills and valleys of Jesus' grimaced brow. This is it. Tonight, at long last, the battle for Jerusalem will begin. Jesus needs you tonight, Peter tells himself. Keep your guard; do not fall asleep.

Jesus heads off into the trees and bushes, and the moment he disappears from sight, all his composure crumbles. His legs give way and Jesus crashes to the ground, kicking up a tower of dust. Dragging his face through the dirt, scraping his fingers through the ground, Jesus lets out a thunderous terrifying howl, sending birds flapping in the treetops.

Jesus is foaming at the mouth. *'Abba, Father! You can do all things. Take away this cup of suffering* (Mark 14:36).'

Ruach clings onto Abba, never letting go. Tears stream from their eyes.

There will be blood.
Jesus' blood.
And it is negotiated.

Jesus' sweat has turned blood red (Luke 22:44). It looks like every blood vessel will burst through his skin. Straining for every breath, Jesus gasps, *'yet not what I will, but what you will* (Mark 14:36*).'
Not what I want.
What you want.
Surrounded by a paradise of greenery the first humans rejected Elohim's will. Instead they chose what they thought was best. They chose what they desired. And they tore a schism between humanity and their passionate Creator, scarring the beauty that surrounded.
Not what I will.
What you will.
Surrounded by a paradise of greenery, Jesus surrenders.
He utters the bravest, most important words of all time.
For the restoration of paradise.
For the renewal of relationship.
There will be blood.
Jesus' blood.
And it is chosen.

Jesus repeats his cry with increasing vigour long into the night. By the time he returns to his followers the dust of the ground is pummelled into his fists, ingrained in his elbows and knees, and flung across his face.
The ground rumbles.
Peter stirs from his slumber. His eyes open to an approaching orange glow, and in a flash he is on his feet, positioned offensively, sword piercing the air in front. Emerging through the trees with torches blazing is a band of armoured soldiers.
Next to the soldiers stand several Jewish priests.

And in front of them all: Judas.

Judas. Judas.

'Ahhhhhhhh,' Peter lunges forward, swinging wildly.

Metal crashes into metal in a frenetic melee.

'*Stop! No more of this* (Luke 22:51).'

Jesus' roar cuts through the night.

'*Put your sword away!* (John 18:11) *All who use swords will be killed with swords* (Matt. 26:52).'

Peter looks into his master's eyes in utter bewilderment.

'*Surely,* Peter, *you know I could ask my Father, and he would give me more than twelve armies of angels* (Matt. 26:52-53).'

Peter's shoulders fall in surrender. His weapon slowly slips from his hand.

Ruach clings onto Jesus, never letting go. She kisses his forehead, his cheeks, his nose, his lips. 'I love you Jesus. I am with you, my dear. *In the last days* (Is. 2:2) our loved ones *will make their swords into ploughs and their spears into hooks for trimming trees. Nations will no longer fight any other nations* (Is. 2:4).

'In the last days there will be no more bloodshed, conflict or massacre. Every sword will have been put away.'

5.10 - Kingdoms on Earth

Ratio, rhythm and routine are rooted in the very essence of the created order. But even for the sun, so accustomed to daily ritual, today will be no ordinary day.

The first morning rays, and the crow of a cockerel, announce the arrival of Jerusalem's annual Passover festival. The city wakes with excitement. Children rush into the streets, dancing and singing, expressing a joy so universal even Roman soldiers cannot stifle a smile.

High Priest Caiaphas however, does not feel like smiling.

His interrogation of Jesus has gone on throughout the night. And until now, all attempts to pin convincing convicting evidence on Jesus have simply resulted in a conflicting web of contradictions.

Caiaphas can stomach it no more. The High Priest rises to his feet and bears down on his prisoner. With an aggravated snap, the Priest yells in Jesus' face, *'Are you the Christ, the Son of the blessed God?* (Mark 14:61)'

Intercepting the text, an arrow branches off from the High Priest's question. We follow the arrow toward a vision seen by the prophet Daniel.

'In my vision,' wrote Daniel, *'there was one like a son of man, coming with the clouds of heaven. He approached the Ancient of Days and was led into his presence. He was given authority, glory and sovereign power; all peoples, nations and men of every language worshipped him. His dominion is an everlasting dominion that will not pass away, and his kingdom is one that will never be destroyed (Dan. 7:13-14*).'*

We read it through carefully, not wanting to miss anything. In this vision, a human, one like a son of man, is led into the presence of Yahweh. This human is then given reign over the earth like Yahweh. He is worshipped as if he is Yahweh himself.

'My face became white from fear (Dan. 7:28),' said Daniel.

He had seen the ultimate blasphemy.

'Are you going to answer? I'll ask you one final time. Are you the Christ?'

In solid defiance, Jesus leans closer into Caiaphas' face.

'*I am. And in the future you will see the Son of Man sitting at the right hand of God, the Powerful One, and coming on clouds in the sky* (Mark 14:62).'

Fury explodes.

Fists and saliva fly into Jesus.

'Kill him!' the High Priest screeches, tearing his clothes in great distress. No further evidence is needed; he has heard the ultimate blasphemy.

And the day's first drop of blood drips to the floor.

'But, but...' we stutter desperately. 'This isn't blasphemy. This is truth. Jesus was conceived by the breath of Ruach. He is divine. He can enter God's presence. He will reign victorious. He will reign over his kingdom on earth.'

Nobody seems able to hear us.

Lost in the silence, we feel totally confused. We feel convinced that Jesus is about to accomplish the Rescue Mission's greatest, most important victory. Yet we have no idea how. Yes, Jesus is the new covenant. Yes, Jesus will shed some of his blood for the forgiveness of sins, putting an end to the punishments that Justice demands, guaranteeing an era of God's everlasting kindness.

But forgiveness won't do it all; forgiveness won't ensure an everlasting paradise. Forgiveness won't stop humans from messing up over and over again, continually diminishing the beauty of the new kingdom. The first humans rejected their Creator's desire and ate from the forbidden tree of the knowledge of good and evil. Ever since, their descendants have done the same, over and over and over again.

Jesus' kingdom must be free from all temptation.

Paradise must contain no knowledge of good and evil.

All evil must be purged; defeated and destroyed once and for all.

At the climax of Daniel's vision, after the words, 'his kingdom is one that will never be destroyed,' another arrow branches off and leads us towards a narrative of Jesus in the desert, to the time when he spent forty days in the desert without food or water.

'*Then the devil took Jesus and showed him all the kingdoms of the world in an instant.*'

We freeze. Devil? Who is this devil?

'The devil said to Jesus, "I will give you all these kingdoms and all their power and glory. It has been given to me, and I can give it to anyone I wish. If you worship me, then it will be yours (Luke 4:5-7)."'

Who is this devil who possesses kingdoms on Earth?

The arrows on the wall keep coming; they seem to be forming a trail. Another directs us towards a story which Jesus told: *'The kingdom of heaven is like a man who planted good seed in a field. That night, when everyone was asleep, his enemy came and planted weeds among the wheat (Matt. 13:24-25).'* Jesus then explained, *'The field is the world, and the good seeds are all of God's children who belong to the kingdom... and the enemy who planted the bad seed is the devil (Matt. 13:38-39).'*

The devil is the enemy, the enemy of God, the tempter in the garden, planter of bad seed; the one who tempts humans away from choosing life.

Creation has been hijacked.

Blindfolded.

Tied up and held to ransom.

This is the horrific, despicable work of the Hijacker.

The Hijacker has stolen power, stolen dominion over the earth.

The Hijacker parades and marauds, wickedly licking his lips, revelling in his possession.

It is not the Romans that Jesus is confronting.

Jesus is fighting the Hijacker's kingdom.

And the continuing trail of arrows reveals that Jesus has been winning every battle fought so far. Upon straightening the back of a crippled woman, Jesus told disapproving priests: *'This woman that I healed, a daughter of Abraham, has been held by Satan for eighteen years (Luke 13:16).'*

The devil; Satan; Beelzebub: literally, 'The Lord of the Flies.'

Demon by demon, Jesus has been overthrowing the Hijacker, and restoring the kingdom of God (Luke 11:20). Demon by demon, Satan has been falling like lightning from the heavens (Luke 10:18).

But individual victories will not be enough.

Jesus needs to deliver a definitive knock-out blow.

The Hijacker's kingdom must be destroyed for evermore.

Only then will paradise reign.

5.11 - For He Has Won

Caiaphas may want to kill Jesus, but the more we think about it the less we are concerned. The more perilous Jesus' plight, the more dramatic his escape, the more memorable his rescue: that's how the Rescue Mission works, isn't it? Phase Three's Egyptian liberation wouldn't still be emblazoned on our memory if Pharaoh had just let the Israelites go when Moses first asked, if the Israelites hadn't seemed doomed to destruction before the waves parted.

The wall tells us that Jesus cannot be executed without Roman sanction. And blasphemy isn't even a crime under Roman law; the Empire promotes the notion of gods in human flesh. Jesus' execution will only be authorised if Caiaphas can prove that he is a political threat, a potent revolutionary.

But Jesus hasn't even swung a sword yet.

Instead he has roared, 'Put away your sword.'

There's no doubt in our mind: Jesus will not be killed.

'You brought this man to me saying he makes trouble among the people,' Roman Governor Pilate announces to the swarming masses gathered below his balcony. *'But I have questioned him before you all, and I have not found him guilty of what you say (Luke 23:14).'*

There is an audible intake of breath, before complete and utter bedlam. Fists shake in derision and within seconds missiles are being thrown at Pilate's majestic palace.

Pilate cannot understand it. He has just acquitted one of the crowd's own, pardoned a Jewish challenger of Rome; they should be celebrating. Yet Pilate can see the hatred in Caiaphas' eyes; he is whipping up this storm. For some reason, and Pilate has no idea why, this man needs Jesus dead.

The irony is not lost on Pilate. His act of exonerating Jesus from starting an uprising could have inadvertently started an uprising. In no time at all, this riot could disseminate into chaos and a bloody crackdown on the Jewish populous. And at Passover as well; how would that look?

Pilate rolls his eyes. He is cornered with no room for manoeuvre.

Jesus will have to be punished severely.

But he will not be killed.

Pilate could never allow such an injustice.

Throughout it all Jesus stands motionless, heart beating with passionate love. Residing in human flesh, Yahweh stares straight into the eyes of his people, seeing only contempt, disdain and derision all around. After millennia of conveying his affection here Love stands receiving nothing but the vilest hatred. His back tenses and straightens preparing for the physical agony about to join the emotional suffering already underway.

There will be blood.

Jesus' blood.

And it is chosen.

As if positioned for prayer - and he most probably is - Jesus kneels with hands tied to a post, his naked body shuddering even before the first lashing connects. When the first thwack strikes bare back, the sensation isn't just one of leather throbbing. Instead each shard of metal clings like claws in multiple places. Having taken hold they dig deep then tug.

And scrape.

And rip.

And tear.

Hurling chunks of flesh to the floor below.

Blood quickly follows, spraying out in a parabola.

And again.

And again.

Soon Jesus kneels in a pool of his own blood and flesh.

Eyes shut tighter than they've ever been shut before. Only images of loved ones in the mind keep Jesus upright.

Cling. Mother, brothers and sisters, this is for you.

Tug. For each precious friend: those watching on distraught; those who have fled in fear.

Tear. For you Abba, for you Ruach.

With teeth clenched so tight they grind, he can hold it in no longer. The audible manifestation of agony shoots from the throat: short, sharp shrieks followed by the exhausted heavy panting, as though of a dog; then one long howl.

154

Kneeling in a puddle of our own tears, hands clenched tightly together in front, we flinch as each blow of the whip grips, rips and shreds Jesus. 'MAKE IT STOP!' we shout. 'Make it stop. That's enough. There's enough.' With our voice hurting to the point of disuse we plead on, 'There's enough. Rescuer, do something, now.'

As if responding to our cry, a piece of paper floats down from the Phase Four rafters, rocking back and forth through the air. We intercept its fall and open up a note written by Isaiah. *'I offered my back to those who beat me* (Is. 50:6),' it says.

Our head shakes in bewilderment.

'Stop now. Please. There's enough. Surely there's enough blood here for the new covenant. STOP! Surely there's enough for the forgiveness of sins.'

With every patch of bare skin on the back either ripped off or hidden under a coating of dripping blood, the whippings finally stop. A kick to the ribs sends the seething pain of his open wounds so high that Jesus feels on fire. A crown made of thorny branches is shoved onto his head, piercing the skin at various places, causing parallel lines of red blood to trickle down over Jesus' forehead.

Now there's enough.
Now it has finished.
Surely.
Please, Abba, please.

Jesus' shattered limp body is dragged in front of the Passover crowds again, and placed next to a bulky slobbering brute named Barabbas. Pilate will offer the crowds a choice. One of these men will be freed as a goodwill Passover offering (John 18:39).

It's the unpunished but guilty versus the mutilated but innocent.

It's violence against non-violence.

Murder or surrender.

'I have Barabbas and Jesus. Which do you want me to set free for you?'

'Barabbas.'

'So what should I do with Jesus, the one you call Christ?'

'Crucify him!'

'Why? What wrong has he done?'
'Crucify him! (Matt. 27:21-23)'
Their yelling becomes *so loud that Pilate* decides *to give them what they* want. *He* sets *free the man… in jail for rioting and murder, and he* hands *Jesus over… to do with him as they* wish (Luke 23:23-25).

We cannot cope with the suspense any longer. Angered by the insanity of it all, feeling like we are going to be sick, we are just desperate to learn of Jesus' fate, desperate to discover how Jesus will be rescued.

Our eyes flick down the wall and skip a large chunk of narrative.

It was about noon and the whole land became dark until three o'clock in the afternoon because the sun did not shine. Then *Jesus cried out in a loud voice, 'Father, I give you my life.'*
After Jesus said this, he died (Luke 23:44-46).

Shaking our head with mouth wide open we stumble back, only to lose our footing and crash to the floor. No, no, no, it cannot be. A split second before our eyes follow suit, the room plunges into darkness. Our body runs cold; vomit falls from our mouth.

Never before have we felt so distraught, so afraid, so vulnerable, so alone.

Because with God's ultimate plan slaughtered… there will be… no… rescue.

The Mission has failed.

And the Hijacker skips and jumps with wicked glee, for he has won.

5.12 - When Darkness Rules

Staring straight up into a black abyss, we have lain flat on the floor for what could be over an hour by now. Arms and legs spread out like a star, in a trance-like state, our body lies motionless and numb, absent of all emotion.

As the minutes trudge slowly by, ever so gradually our senses return. It is freezing cold, we lie soaking in a puddle, and we can smell our own vomit. Full of pain, we choose to return to our trance. At least it is safe there. At least it hurts less there.

'This is your time - the time when darkness rules (Luke 22:53).'

A loud but fractured voice shakes us from our daze.

Wondering whether we are no longer alone, we lift our head upright for the first time in hours. Pitch-black and bitter cold engulfs us. And only now does an aching, distressed, almost childlike groan come, bringing with it the first fresh wave of tears. Rolling up into a ball, clutching our neck, dragging hands through our hair, our mourning begins.

'It's all over' we bellow again and again, between heavy, rasping breaths. Grieving the end of hope, we thump the ground in anger, discovering that the freezing temperatures have turned our pool of tears to ice.

Because dignity no longer matters, we take hold of our clothing and start to rip.

And tear.

And shred.

Clunk, clunk.

The sound is of something metallic falling to the ice. Scrambling in the dark, we locate a small cylindrical torch, fallen from our ripped pocket. This is the torch that successfully - but now pointlessly - guided us through the Phase Four loft.

We switch the instrument on, and our eyes battle to adjust. Although blurred by our tears, we are able to make out numerous scraps of paper scattered over the iced floor. Clambering on our knees and elbows over the slippery surface, we pick up each scrap. And for several minutes we just sit there, papers in hand, refusing to engage.

Why should we?

It's just not worth it any more.

It's all over.

But eventually.

Eventually.

Eventually the silence and boredom become too much.

With a heavy heart, we lay out the pieces of paper in front of us and glimpse over them. Before long, we notice that the pieces can be placed into two piles: those 'Written by David' - lyrics from a song, we assume - and those 'By Isaiah.'

We take a deep breath. Convinced that only further misery awaits, we summon the courage to engage with our grief and shine the torch towards the Phase Five wall.

We illuminate the text that we skipped: the final hours of Jesus' life.

Outside the city walls of Jerusalem, at a place fittingly known as 'The Skull,' Jesus hangs on two wooden beams, his arms spread out on the horizontal, legs dropping down on the vertical. For every intake of breath, Jesus can only use his arms to lift his body up. The motion is so excruciating, exhaustion will be the most likely cause of death; that's if blood loss or dehydration doesn't strike first.

Shining the torch down to the paper in our hand, we read, 'My heart is like wax; it has melted inside me. My strength has dried up like a clay pot, and my tongue sticks to the top of my mouth (Ps. 22:14-15).'

And Jesus gasps, 'I am thirsty (John 19:28).'

The agony of the simple statement brings another wave of weeping from portions of the watching crowds, particularly Jesus' mother. But for others it brings much comedy. They are relishing their power, enjoying crushing the one who claimed such greatness, revelling in his fall from grace.

That the sorry, repulsive figure suspended in front of them does nothing proves he is no king. Jesus is no Messiah. They mock and taunt and hurl insults, urging Jesus to save himself. Yet still Jesus hangs.

King David writes, '*But I am like a worm instead of a man. People make fun of me and hate me... They say, "Turn to* Yahweh *for help. Maybe he will save you (Ps. 22:8)."'*

We double-take, as the seed of a formidable possibility drops into our heart.

Laughing away amongst themselves, soldiers sit competing for a memento from their day's achievements. They throw lots to win Jesus' bloodied clothes.

The next paper in our hand reads, '*They divided my clothes among them, and they threw lots for my clothing (Ps. 22:18).*'

Our head shakes in shock.

Surely not.

It cannot be.

We check the next piece.

'*They have pierced my hands and feet (Ps. 22:16*).*'

No way. No way. This is too much to take in. Three large nails attach Jesus to the wooden beams. Two pierce the base of his hands. One is hammered through his feet.

No way. This is incredible. Did David really write about this day, centuries before crucifixion was even conceived?

With physical, emotional and spiritual persecution firing through every sinew of his being, Jesus carefully chooses words to express and encapsulate his most throbbing wound.

To do so he lifts the words directly from David's lyrics:

'*My God, my God, why have you rejected me? (Ps. 22:1)*'

The most throbbing wound is rejection.

Disconnection crushes the heart.

Jesus feels abandoned.

Abandoned by Love.

Abandoned by Abba.

When separation from the one who breathes life comes, life cannot go on.

Jesus roars in agony then breathes out for the final time.

Our body shakes in an eruption of pent-up pain. Absorbed by the Rescuer's constant longing for relationship we connect with the ultimate disconnection.

We mourn separation.

We weep for Jesus' loss.

A Roman soldier approaches the limp body, and like a butcher in a slaughterhouse, stabs his spear into the flesh.

'This is your time - the time when darkness rules.'

The same stilted, struggling, strained voice fills the Headquarters. The voice is strikingly real. It is not in our head. It is with us, around us, surrounding us, moving us to tears.

'They will look on me, the one they have stabbed, and they will cry like someone crying over the death of an only child. They will be as sad as someone who has lost a firstborn son (Zech. 12:10).'

We weep for Abba's loss.

5.13 - There Can Be No Relationship

On either side of Jesus' motionless, spiritless frame, two convicted criminals cling frantically to their final moments of life. Approaching each offender with metal in hand, soldiers pummel the men's legs, smashing and cracking until they hear the legs shatter (John 19:32).

The men scream through gritted teeth. They can no longer lift themselves to breathe. They shall be dead in moments.

The soldiers turn to face Jesus.

They do not need to *break his legs.*

He is *already dead* (John 19:33).

Having worked our way through the lyrics of David, we turn to the second pile of papers in our hands, those 'By Isaiah.' *'He was beaten down and punished,'* the first piece reads, *'but he didn't say a word. He was like a lamb being led to be killed* (Is. 53:7).'

Our head bows. This prophecy, written seven centuries before Jesus' death, sufficiently describes Jesus' surrender. An annotation on the paper explains that the lamb eaten during the annual Passover feasts was always without fault. It was always unmarked, with no broken bones.

The threads pull together in our mind.

Killed at Passover, slaughtered like a lamb, with no broken bones: was... was... was Jesus' death deliberately like that of a Passover lamb?

'He was buried with wicked men... He had done nothing wrong, and he had never lied (Is. 53:9).'

We nod in recognition. Jesus was unmarked, unblemished, completely without fault. He was the ultimate, definitive Passover lamb.

During the Egyptian liberation, God saw the blood of a lamb painted on Israelite doorframes, and judgment and death passed over them. Was the original Passover a model, a sign, a forerunner of something far greater? Has Jesus' death always been part of the Rescue Mission's long term plan?

Was the Messiah's mission to die?

Was Jesus' life destined to death?

Isaiah asserts, 'But it was Yahweh who decided to crush him and make him suffer (Is. 53:10).'

'But... but... but...' we stutter, before breaking down again. The thought is just too much to take in. The question, finally forced out through tearful splutters, is too much to contemplate: 'But why?'

Soaked wet by our tears, we look down at the next Isaiah quotation. Sensing its contents, we almost dare not look, dreading a devastating truth.

'He took our suffering on him and felt our pain for us (Is. 53:4).'

For us.

Jesus took the punishment: for us.

He took the death that we deserve.

That we deserve.

Like a volcanic eruption, memories explode up from our depths.

Memories of thoughts which smothered beauty with dirt.

Words which suffocated life.

Actions which smacked against justice.

And most of all, for we have even done it in this room, we are struck by our constant ignoring and denial of God's presence, our rejection of love, our rejection of relationship.

It is sin which holds Jesus to the wooden beams.

The world's sin.

And our sin.

We killed Jesus.

Falling on to all fours again, we stare down at the iced floor. Torchlight shines on the surface, causing the ice to act as a mirror and reflect back an image of our pallid face. Our eyes are overcome with guilt, the pupils are dilated, the irises bloodshot, all surrounding areas blackened.

Then we notice the blood.

The palms of our hands are dripping.

There's blood on our hands.

'Father.'

A flash of fear shoots through our aching body.

'Father.'

The voice is the one that we heard earlier, the one in the room with us, permeating through us. Fearing judgement and condemnation, retribution and punishment, we peer nervously upward.

'Father, forgive them, because they do not know what they are doing (Luke 23:34*).'

Our head drops down to the ice. Only one word is on our mind. It rumbles around inside of us, increasing in energy before spewing out: 'Sorry.'

Again and again we spit out the word; each repetition flowing increasingly free: 'Sorry. Sorry.'

What happens next is a sight we shall never forget. The dark stains surrounding our eyes gradually lift and colour returns to our cheeks. We slowly lift our hands up to our eye-line and stare straight into our palms.

The blood has gone.

Eyes open wide, face fresh with amazement, we want to thank the voice; we want to see the voice. But silence has returned. We are alone again.

Once more we look down at our hands: they are still clean. And dropped down on the ice beside us, we spot one final extract from Isaiah. *'He willingly gave his life,'* Isaiah writes, *'and was treated like a criminal. But he carried away the sins of many people and asked forgiveness for those who sinned* (Is. 53:12).'

Having felt the invigorating touch of forgiveness, we rise to our feet and return to the Phase Five wall. A seed of hope is germinating within us: perhaps Jesus' death isn't the end after all?

In Jerusalem's Temple, an enormous, majestic curtain lies crumpled in a heap. For almost a thousand years, this glorious embroidered curtain had served as a blockade, protecting dirt-stained humans from perishing in God's beautiful, spotless holiness. Apart from one man, once a year, when entering with blood as an offering for sin, no-one was allowed beyond the curtain and into the Temple's Most Holy Place.

Ripped from top to bottom - a miraculous feat in itself - the demise of the blockade took place at exactly the moment that Jesus died (Matt. 27:51). Jesus *entered the Most Holy Place only once - and for all time. He did not take with him the blood of goats and calves. His sacrifice was his own blood and by it he set us free from sin forever* (Heb. 9:12).

Thanks to Jesus' ultimate offering, now all can enter into God's spotless, beautiful presence; because they are spotless and beautiful too.

We want to put our hands in the air to dance and celebrate: this is the breakthrough, the advancement that God has craved for millennia. But how can we possibly dance when darkness still surrounds?

When darkness rules, there can be no relationship.

The Hijacker still reigns victorious.

Because Elohim remains dead in the grave.

5.14 - Both Hug Tight

With the lip quivering, like it will give way at any moment, Thomas sits crumpled in a corner, cutting a bitter and twisted figure. This devastated disciple of Jesus is beyond tears; they've all been buried deep inside beneath a pile of resentment and regret.

Thomas has been counting the days since hope was executed. Today is Monday. Ten agony filled days have passed since everything truly worth living for was snatched from before his eyes. He'd truly believed that Jesus could overthrow the Romans. The miracles - and even the words - had been so convincing.

Maybe Jesus believed it too? He always seemed so sincere.

Maybe Jesus fell for his own hype as well?

Instead of resenting Jesus, Thomas blames himself. This entire nightmare could have been spared if he'd just stopped Jesus getting too ambitious.

Alongside the head spinning muddle of analysis, Thomas is also mourning the tragic loss of a great friend. Nobody so young, nobody so innocent, deserves to die like that.

But it's all over now.

It has finished.

This was no Messiah.

In the same room, the other ten members of Jesus' inner circle sit together separate from Thomas. In the last week, Thomas has seen each one completely lose the plot. The grief has sent them insane. A week ago they all claim to have seen Jesus alive.

Like, actually alive!

It's only natural, Thomas muses, to see what you want to see when mourning.

Peter and John defend their insanity, arguing that Jesus' tomb is empty. But that means nothing; the body could have been stolen.

And Mary Magdalene even claims to have had a one-to-one conversation with him. But she's always been a touch crazy.

Again and again, with incessant excitement and animation, the other followers have told Thomas, *'We saw the Lord* (John 20:25).'

Refusing to believe may leave Thomas increasingly isolated and ignored, but he is going nowhere. As the only one left of sound mind he must keep them safe, and ensure everyone keeps a low profile until their crazed spell wears off. All failed revolutionaries could well be the next targets on the Roman hit list.

Thomas double checks again: the doors are locked.

They are safe.

'*I will not believe it until I see the nail marks in his hands and put my finger where the nails were* (John 20:25).' The sentence has run through Thomas' mind on loop, ever since he first angrily snapped each word with great assertiveness.

Tightly clutching bent knees close to his chest, he whispers the words again:

'I will not believe. Until...'

All of a sudden Thomas sees everyone jump to their feet as the volume rapidly rises.

'What is it now?' he shrugs with frustration, struggling to fathom out the fuss.

And then he sees it.

He sees him.

Jesus stands in the room.

In sheer disbelief, Thomas looks to the locked doors: how? This isn't possible. No-one can enter the room.

Despite rising to his feet for further inspection, Thomas has already made up his mind over the mystery. This figure looking like Jesus must be a ghost or some sort of mirage, which means he too has finally been infected with insanity.

Thomas moves closer. His peripheral vision fades into irrelevance as he finds himself increasingly mesmerized by a figure of overwhelming beauty, and definite likeness to Jesus.

But Jesus had never been one blessed with good looks.

This could be a ghost.

I will not believe.

Until I see.

Until I touch.

Love radiates from Jesus' radiant eyes, and Thomas feels every knot inside begin to loosen. A warm glowing sensation takes over the pit of his stomach, which spreads rapidly through his whole body when Jesus opens his mouth and familiar, much missed tones are heard.

'Put your finger here, and look at my hands (John 20:27).'

A champion's smile beams at Thomas, as Jesus holds out his hands.

Revealing nail scarred wrists.

Fingers gently caress Jesus' forearm, slowly stroking down towards his hand; but before reaching the palm they slide effortlessly into, and find rest within, the hole.

Thomas looks up, his face a picture of amazement, wonder and awe.

And Jesus continues to smile knowingly.

Taking hold of both wrists, placing a thumb into each crevice, Thomas smiles back. His inner mountain of resentment and regret crumbles away, freeing access for a tear of joy to trickle down.

After a couple of minutes, a fully settled and certain Thomas loosens his grip from the wrists, allowing Jesus to reach upward and tenderly wipe the tear from his friend's cheek before embracing.

Both hug tight.

This can be no ghost.

Thomas can have no doubt.

Because it is true: Jesus is alive.

After the most brutal, torturous death, Jesus is alive.

Where death had triumphed, life now bursts forth to deliver the knockout blow.

Evil kicks and screams in writhing agony.

Because, with the Hijacker's ultimate achievement comprehensively conquered, there will be rescue.

The Mission has succeeded.

And Yahweh jumps and dances and embraces with sheer delight and ecstasy, for he has won.

5.15 - Completing Phase Five

Into the darkness of night a light rises. The golden sunbeams of daybreak reflect off Lake Galilee's surface, causing it to shimmer and shine. On the water, a small fishing vessel is floating calmly. On board, two friends stand staring out at the stunning horizon, basking in the rays of rising sun. 'That's how I felt when I saw him,' Thomas grins at Peter. 'His light overcame my darkness (Eph. 5:8).'

Hands land forcefully on the pair's shoulders, dramatically interrupting the peace. Behind them John is jumping and shouting like an excited child: '*It is the Lord!* (John 21:7) It is the Lord!'

John is pointing across the water and sure enough, Peter and John can see the figure standing on the shore. And without a moment's hesitation - for he's never been one to think before acting - Peter has leapt into the lake. His frenetic swimming to the shore brings the entire crew much amusement.

Jesus is laughing too, standing with arms open wide ready to usher in the soaking wet fisherman.

As Peter approaches the shore he notices fish frying on *a fire of hot coals* (John 21:9).

Jesus is preparing breakfast on the beach.

With the meal of bread and cooked fish consumed to full satisfaction, the Rescuer can hold it in no more; Jesus is simply desperate to ask his friends a question, one burning deep within.

It's a question that Yahweh has been asking for millennia. It's a question that has been beating with fervent passion at the very core of Love. And now, thanks to Jesus' ultimate triumph, the entire Rescue Mission has been stripped to its heartbeat.

Jesus wants to ask, '*Do you love me?* (John 21:16)'

PHASE SIX

6.01 - Let There Be Light

In the beginning there was the Word.
The Word was with God and the Word was God (John 1:1).
In the beginning, *the earth was formless and empty* (Gen. 1:2).
Then the Word spoke into the darkness, *'Let there be light.'*
And there was light (Gen. 1:3).
The Word was in the world.
And the world was made by him.
But the world did not know him.
So *the Word* took on flesh.
The Word *became human* (John 1:14).
And chose to dwell with the centrepiece of his creation.

Wherever the Word breathed, beauty arose. His every word brought revelation and healing, equality and forgiveness. Eyes opened to the possibility of a whole new way of living. Minds awakened to the prospect of a better world.

Right from the beginning, from the moment Ruach first breathed life into humans, Love has sought collaboration and relationship. Seeing *everything that he had made* and calling it *'very good,'* Elohim decided to rest from creating (Gen. 1:31-2:2). Instead, humans were invited to share creative responsibility.

'Be fruitful and increase in number,' was Elohim's passionate plea. *'Fill the earth and subdue it. Rule over the fish in the sea and the birds in the air and over every living creature* (Gen. 1:28).'

Crafted in the image of their Creator, humans were invited to create new life.

They were commissioned to cultivate, nurture and conserve.
Every act of construction.
Distribution.
Education.
Development.

Management.

Organisation.

Administration.

It all serves to bring order to chaos.

And now the time has come for the resurrected Jesus to add to the original creation mandate. Standing with his followers on the mountaintops, the air bracing, the view expansive, Jesus stretches his arms to the skies and gently commands, '*You will be my witnesses in Jerusalem, in all Judea and Samaria, and to the ends of the earth* (Acts 1:9). *All authority in heaven and earth has been given to me. Therefore go and make disciples of all nations* (Matt. 28:18-19).'

At the dawn of a new creation, *the firstborn from among the dead* (Col. 1:18) invites his followers to share creative responsibility. Equipped with every power in the universe, Love seeks collaboration and relationship.

'*I am the light of the world* (John 8:12),' Jesus declares, before leaning forward into the ear of his Bride, and whispering, '*You are the light of the world* (Matt. 5:14*). Now let there be light!'

At that Jesus' resurrected body leaves the ground and rises into the air.

Clouds gather around him.

And then he is gone, visible no more.

At first, Peter's instinctive response was to grieve for Jesus all over again. His master, his friend, his life's purpose, had left him again. But as the days passed, Jesus' parting words began to soothe and massage, then invigorate and energise.

Now Peter stands as the epitome of expectation. Ten days on from Jesus' ascension, Peter sways from side to side, bold and brash, imploring his friends to stay strong.

'We saw Daniel's vision - the Son of Man journeying on the clouds - we saw it plain before our very eyes. That's how we can be sure that Jesus is reigning with all "*authority, glory and power*" (Dan. 7:14).'

Peter's arms swing with excitement.

'The wait is nearly over. Jesus promised that he would ask the Father to provide a *Counsellor to be with* us *forever* (John 14:16*). *When the Holy Spirit comes, we will receive power* (Acts 1:8).'

No one in the room dares disagree. Their lives are on hold until the Breath of God arrives. Not even the raucous celebrations of Pentecost, blaring from the streets below, will distract them from their focus.

Waiting.

Waiting.

Waiting.

Suddenly a sound like a violent wind (Acts 2:2) crashes through the house. Ruach rushes and swirls, shaking those in her midst, igniting what looks like flames. Then, like she did in the very first humans, like she did in Moses' tabernacle and Solomon's Temple, Ruach enters, settles down and makes herself at home; Jesus' followers become *the temple of the living God* (2 Cor. 6:16).

Fifty days ago, Jesus died and rose again at Passover - the annual celebration of Israel's Egyptian liberation. Today, Ruach has descended at Pentecost, the annual celebration of Israel receiving Yahweh's laws; laws that would help a new, emerging, liberated society to flourish.

Every year at Pentecost the first fruit of the year's harvest would be offered to Yahweh.

This year it is Yahweh who makes the offering.

Love.

Joy.

Peace.

Patience.

Kindness.

Goodness.

Faithfulness.

Gentleness.

Self-control (Gal. 5:22-23).

The fruit of Ruach will help a new, emerging, liberated society to flourish. Working in intimate collaboration and relationship, her character inside lives will transform lives.

Abba holds Jesus under his right arm and kisses his Son in pure tender affection. A stunning serenade surrounds, singing over and over: '*The Lamb who was killed is worthy to receive power, wealth, wisdom and strength, honour, glory and praise!* (Rev. 5:12)'

Delight soars within Father and Son as they watch Peter, totally transformed from the fisherman they once knew, bellow to the bustling Pentecost crowds, *'God raised Jesus from the dead* (Acts 2:2).'

Jews from all over the world have journeyed to Jerusalem for the Pentecost festivities; allowing the mission of Phase Six to begin with Jews from Egypt, Arabia, Mesopotamia, Asia, Crete, even Rome, all responding to Peter's call to, *'Change your hearts and lives and be baptised, each one of you... receive the Holy Spirit* (Acts 2:38).'

Abba's heart is leaping for joy. It summersaults in elation as his new society, overflowing with the fruit of Ruach, starts to reflect his own character. Justice and equality, compassion and generosity all come to the fore, with possessions being shared by rich and poor alike (Acts 2:45).

At the entrance to Jerusalem's Temple, a beggar stops Peter and asks him for money. Peter instantly recognises the man; this beggar is famous for never having walked a step in his life.

'By the power of Jesus,' Peter says with confidence, *'stand up and walk!* (Acts 3:6)'

It's as if new life is breathed into the man's ankles as he jumps to his feet (Acts 3:8) and takes his first steps on the earth.

This is restoration.

This is new life sprouting up.

This is the new creation blossoming, growing up from within the old.

This is the Word speaking into the darkness, 'Let there be Light!'

And there is light.

6.02 - Crown of Flowers

At the very moment that we read of Thomas touching the holes in Jesus' wrists, glorious light filled the Headquarters, illuminating every corner of the room. We peer down at the final piece of Phase Four prophecy in our hand: '*After his soul suffers many things,*' Isaiah declared, '*he will see life and be satisfied* (Is. 53:11).'

Stretching our arms out in triumph we spin round on the spot, basking in the light, marvelling at the entire Rescue Mission. These feel like the first moments of love: the instant attraction, the free-flowing conversation, the look in the eyes, the hours feeling like minutes; if only it could last like this forever.

As warmth returns to the room, the ice beneath our feet begins to melt. Before long, the water is evaporating, lifting with it decades of dust and dirt up from the floor, revealing beneath further hand-written narratives splayed out across the Headquarters floor.

And painted bright in the centre of it all, imprinted at the heart of Phase Six, Jesus promises, '*Because I live, you will live too* (John 14:19).'

With a ragged damp cloth, John gently dabs the congealing wounds strewn across Peter's back; a mottled patchwork of red, blue and black. It is like dousing a bed of sizzling coals. The water cools and stings in equal measure.

'The persecution is getting worse, Peter. Next time, we might not escape with only a beating. Next time they could...'

A knock at the door cuts John short.

'Ignore it,' John urges.

But Peter is already on his feet, striding as best as he can across the room.

'Who is it?' Peter whispers through the doorframe.

'It's me, Philip. I got here as soon as I could. I kept hidden. They didn't see me.'

Peter's relief dissolves the second he opens the door. John sees it too and immediately stands to his feet. Grief is etched across Philip's face.

'It's chaos out there,' Philip chokes. 'They're seizing us all over Jerusalem... And Stephen... Stephen...'

Peter and John look away, fearing the worst.

'Stephen... they killed him.'

'No!'

'They ran at him screaming, they grabbed him like... like... like a bloody slab of meat. They dragged him out of Jerusalem and stoned him.'

'No!' Peter buckles forward, winded.

'But... but... why? What had he done?'

'It was blasphemy. Stephen said the same thing that Jesus said at his trial.'

'*In the future,*' says John, recalling Jesus' inflammatory words, '*you will see the Son of Man sitting at the right hand of God* (Matt. 26:64).'

'Yes, those words exactly. Stephen said that he could see it. He saw "*heaven open and the Son of Man standing at God's right side* (Acts 7:56)." His face was shining in the presence of God. But the priests didn't seem to notice. Or care.'

The three bow their heads.

Together they stand in silence.

Simply paying their respects.

'Why?' Philip asks, brushing away his tears. 'Why are we suffering like this? If Jesus is reigning in glory, possessing every power in the universe, why doesn't he save us?'

Peter and John take their time before responding, choosing their words carefully. 'These are the first days of a whole new world,' Peter begins. 'But these are also *the last days* (Acts 1:14) of the old world.'

'It's as if the old is giving birth to the new,' adds John. 'God's Kingdom has begun. We've seen it: the spirit of God transforming lives. It's here, it's arrived. But it's like Jesus' said: it will be like a seed that grows and grows and grows.'

'*We are waiting for a new heaven and a new earth where goodness lives* (2 Pet. 3:13). Only then will the Kingdom of God be seen in all its fullness.'

'Until then we have been *given the honour of suffering disgrace for Jesus* (Acts 5:41).'

'We must share *in Christ's sufferings* (1 Pet. 4:13). We should follow Jesus' example (1 Pet. 2:21). We should *not repay evil with evil or insult with insult, but with blessing* (1 Pet. 3:9*).'

Listening to the wisdom of his friends, Philip is reminded of Stephen's final dying words. When Stephen cried out, *'Lord, do not hold this sin against them* (Acts 7:60),' he was following Jesus' example. He was echoing Jesus' own dying plea: *'Father, forgive them* (Luke 23:34).'

'But... but...' says Philip, 'what if we all end up dead? What if they kill us all? What good would we be to Jesus then?'

Eyes heavy and piercing, determination and resolve envelope Peter.

'Have faith, Philip. Jesus told us to go to Judea and Samaria, and to the ends of the earth, and he will get us there. God's plans never die. When our ancestors were exiled in Babylon, Jerusalem was in ruins, all hope seemed lost. Yet the King of Babylon was so impressed by our ancestors' faith, he wrote to every nation in his kingdom and decreed, "Israel's God *is the living God; he lives forever. His kingdom will never...* (Dan. 6:26)."'

Crash.

Thrown from its hinges, the front door is sent skidding across the floor. Standing in the doorway is Saul, the most relentless pursuer of Jesus' followers. Saul marches towards them, slashes Peter and John across the face then seizes Philip, pushing a blade up against his throat.

Philip looks Saul in the eye.

And prays blessing on his captor.

Bound in chains, Philip is hurled into the back of a wagon, where he joins hundreds of others captured for allegiance to Jesus (Acts 8:3-4). Saul drives his prisoners to a hurting, barren land, where they can bother Jerusalem no more.

He leaves his exiles in Samaria, the humiliated former capital of Israel.

'How terrible it will be for Samaria, the pride of Israel's drunken people!' Isaiah once prophesied. *'That beautiful crown of flowers is just a dying plant* (Is. 28:1).'

And sure enough, like Jerusalem, Samaria experienced unmitigated annihilation by rampaging enemies.

But unlike Jerusalem, Samaria had never recovered from its destruction.

Unlike Jerusalem, Samaria's exiles had never returned home.

Samaria appeared to have been rejected and abandoned, forever.

That is until today.

Today Philip stands in Samaria and proclaims *the Good News* (Acts 8:12) of Jesus. And hundreds respond to his message. Ruach swoops and swirls in delight, liberating and healing, breathing new life into her returning children, restoring Samaria into a beautiful crown of flowers once again.

6.03 - The Academics of Athens

With the tip of his knife, Saul carefully slices through the fabric in his hand. He sits under the cover of his market-stall shelter, engrossed in his work, almost oblivious to the bustling world around him. Tent making is simply a means to an end for Saul. For thirteen years, he has kept his head down, building his business, earning and saving money, and biding his time.

Rehearsing his proclamations.

Refining his arguments.

Processing his logic.

Preparing his evidence.

Shaping offences.

Structuring defences.

'How much for this one?'

Saul hardly looks up, simply glimpsing the object of enquiry.

'It's fifty for that one.'

'I'll give you a hundred.'

His attention caught, Saul puts his knife down and slowly looks up. A grin stretches across Saul's cheeks as he jumps to his feet, arms open for embrace. 'Barnabas, old friend, how are you? I've not seen you in years.'

'We're doing well thanks, Saul. You'll be pleased to hear, news of Jesus is really spreading.'

'Oh, Barnabas, that is such good news.'

'But we think it's time to go further, Saul - much further. That's why I'm here. We need you, Saul. You're a Roman citizen, you speak Greek, you understand Greek culture, and you know the Jewish scriptures inside out. Oh, and you're from Tarsus - you'll know how to sail.'

'Barnabas,' says Saul, without a moment's hesitation. 'It'd be an absolute honour to travel with you. You were the first to forgive me for pursuing and persecuting you all; it would be a privilege to follow wherever you lead... Just how far were you thinking of going?'

Barnabas flashes his friend a playful smile.

'Let's just say you'd better start using your Roman name.'

'Right you are. I am Paul, at your service.'

Zeus.

Apollo.

Athena.

Neptune.

Ares.

Athena.

Paul walks through the streets of Athens, feeling sick to the stomach, Ruach squirming inside him. He has never seen so many monuments dedicated to gods. It's no exaggeration: there are literally thousands of the things. The city is saturated.

A theatre for Dionysus.

A stadium for Poseidon.

Athena.

Athena.

A temple for Neptune.

An altar '*TO A GOD WHO IS NOT KNOWN* (Acts 17:23).'

Athena.

Athena.

Tears well in Paul's eyes as words of Isaiah clatter back and forth through his mind:

'A man cuts down a tree,
Burns half of the wood in the fire…
He makes a statue from the wood that is left
And calls it his god.
He bows down to it and worships it.
He prays to it and says,
  "You are my God. Save me!"
It's as if their eyes are covered so they can't see.
Their minds don't understand…
They have not thought to themselves…
  "I am worshipping a block of wood! (Is. 44:16-19)"'

Before the days of Isaiah, the prophet Elijah challenged the Canaanite god Baal to set fire to a large pile of wood. The Baal worshippers cut their skin, desperately seeking their god's attention. But after several hours they had failed to summon a single flame.

Elijah then drenched the wood with water, prayed out to Yahweh, and watched a raging fire begin to blaze. '*If Baal really is a god, maybe he is thinking, or busy, or travelling! Maybe he is sleeping* (1 Kings 18:27),' Elijah taunted.

Elijah showed that Baal had no power.

Because Baal was simply a chiselled block of wood.

Just like Zeus, Apollo and Athena.

There really is only one true God.

One great universal God.

Who desires the hearts of every nation.

To God every person is the same (Acts 10:34).

There is no difference between Greeks and Jews (Col 3:11).

The only trouble is: the Greeks are not waiting for a Christ to liberate them.

They do not know the prophecies of Isaiah.

They were never ruled by David.

They were never liberated by Moses.

They were not fathered by Abraham.

How, Paul wonders, can he present Jesus as the climax and fulfilment of a millennia old story, when the people of Athens do not know the story so far?

Worse still, at the heart of Paul's message is a physical, flesh and blood resurrection; Jesus' body returning to life in the same world in which he died. Yet the Greeks believe that only the human soul, not the body, lives on after death, in some other completely spiritual realm.

And then there's the crucifixion - a stumbling block to Jews and Greeks alike (1 Cor. 1:22-23). The Greek mind may be able to accept the notion of a god in human flesh - that's not an alien concept to them - but when Paul reveals that this divine flesh was slaughtered by human hands... well, they will laugh (Acts 17:32).

Because the gods do not suffer.

No god could ever be humiliated like that.

Paul shakes his head, racking his brains for inspiration. Staring up at a giant gold statue of Athena, the goddess of Athens, he doubts whether such deeply engrained beliefs could ever be transformed.

For Paul himself, it was only a miracle of the most astounding proportions which transformed his deeply engrained beliefs. No persuasive argument or personal testimony arrested his mind. It was only the direct intervention of Jesus, engulfing him in an explosion of pure blinding light, hearing Jesus shout, *'Saul, Saul! Why are you persecuting me? (Acts 9:4)'*

Paul has seen Jesus heal a crippled man in Lystra (Acts 14:10).

He has seen Jesus shake the ground in Philippi (Acts 16:26).

And in all cases, it was the experiences coupled with explanation which revolutionised hearts and minds.

But what if there are no remarkable miracles today?

What if Paul is left with only words to convince the Greek intellectuals? What could he say?

Entering Athens' bustling marketplace, Paul gets to work, striking up several conversations. And in a metropolis of ideas, open to change and advancement, a crowd soon gathers around him. Before long, Paul has been invited to present his radical convictions to Athens' most high-profile philosophers, the successors of the world famous Plato, Sophocles and Socrates.

'People of Athens,' Paul begins, Ruach breathing confidence within him, *'I can see you are very religious.* So I want to tell you about the God you do not know - *the God who made the whole world... the One who gives life, breath and everything else* (Acts 17:22-25).'

As he speaks, Paul watches his audience intently.

In Thessalonica, he was hounded out of town.

In Philippi, he was beaten and imprisoned.

What will be the reaction from the academics of Athens?

6.04 - Revolution Is Complete

After three days of non-stop darkness, everything is moving but nothing is rhythmic. It's as if the ship is being thrown around by a sick and twisted nemesis: teasing and tormenting, tossing and turning in jagged pincer movements.

The winds are mighty and merciless.

The waves ride high and crash vehemently.

The rain swirls and lashes, drenching all in its wake.

And men sprint aimlessly, shrieking and screaming in futile panic.

Soldier, sailor or prisoner, all have given up hope (Acts 27:20). Their battered fragile ship is being held together by rope (Acts 27:17). It could shatter any moment, sentencing all to the depths, swallowed up forever by the ravenous seas.

Resting in the arms of his Ruach, an elderly man sits quietly amongst the cargo.

I will make it to Rome, he prays.

I will make it to Rome.

You have promised it, Father (Acts 23:11).

I will meet with Caesar.

I will meet with Caesar.

Ruach gently massages the bald and bearded prisoner, comforting and reassuring, bringing peace to his bones. '*To live is Christ and to die is gain* (Philip. 1:21*),' she whispers. 'But today is not the day that you will die. There is still much for you to do. You will make it to Rome.'

Though chained by his hands, the prisoner pushes down on a barrel and manages to force himself up to his feet. Fighting against the wind and rain, he stumbles forward.

'Stop! Stop!' he roars.

Heads turn on frantic sprinting bodies, and on realising who it is shouting, pandemonium grinds to a halt. All have deep respect for this dishevelled impoverished prisoner. Despite decades of hardships, his warmth and generosity have remained unswerving. They may not always agree with what he says, but whenever Paul speaks, everyone listens.

'Men, listen to me. *Last night an angel came to me* and *said, "Paul, do not be afraid. You must stand trial before Caesar* (Acts 27:24)." So men, *keep up your courage* (Acts 27:22*); *not one of you will die; only the ship will be lost* (Acts 27:22).'

Whenever ships sailed out from the selfish, promiscuous city of Corinth, Paul's contrasting message of faithful, sacrificial love journeyed with them, wherever they sailed. It was all testimony to the success of Paul's strategy: he would focus his efforts on cities with influence and prestige.

Thessalonica was the capital of Macedonia.

Athens was the former capital of the world.

Corinth was a centre of trade for the entire Roman Empire.

And Rome is the hub, the heart, the centre of it all; the capital of the world.

Quite literally, all roads lead to Rome.

From Rome, Jesus' liberation really could spread to the ends of the earth.

Eight centuries ago, Isaiah provocatively prophesied: 'Yahweh *will show himself to the Egyptians, and then they will know he is* Yahweh. *They will worship God* (Is. 19:21).' Isaiah's contemporaries were thoroughly disgusted by the thought of the former enemy, former ruler, former oppressor falling in love with Yahweh.

But here, today, the Community of Elohim leans forward in enthusiastic anticipation, joy exploding in their hearts, as Paul is welcomed into Rome by a thriving community of Romans.

A community of Romans committed and devoted to Jesus.

A community whose *faith is being reported all over the world* (Rom. 1:8*).

Because the enemy.

The ruler.

The oppressor.

It is absolutely astonishing.

They are accepting Jesus' revolution.

Thirty years ago in Jerusalem, the liberating Christ was expected to massacre the Roman enemy. He would be the greatest, mightiest warrior of all time, the ultimate gladiator, an absolute master with the sword.

Yet Jesus roared, 'Put away your sword!'

His words stunned everyone.

And his non-violent approach to revolution was quickly crushed, quashed with sheer ease. He was slaughtered in the name of entertainment, suffering the most gruesome, humiliating, excruciating Roman execution.

Thirty years on, there are Romans in Rome proclaiming that 'Jesus is Lord (Acts 28:15).' Each Roman directly defies and denies Caesar's rule. Each risks retribution for undermining the Empire's ultimate authority.

Walking through the centre of Rome, Paul passes a temple for the Roman god Mars, another for the god Neptune, another for Saturn. And at the top of the hill he sees the largest temple of all, a temple for Jupiter, king of the Roman pantheon. It all reminds Paul of the scene of his greatest disappointment, his failure to convince the academics in Athens nearly two decades ago.

That really was a missed opportunity. With the acceptance and support of the renowned Greek philosophers, who knows how quickly the Good News of Jesus could have spread?

Paul narrows his eyes, Ruach strengthening his resolve.

Soon Paul will meet with Caesar.

And this time, the opportunity shall not pass him by.

If he can just convince Caesar that Jesus is the one true Lord, reigning in glory over all the earth... well, the possibilities are endless. The ends of the earth could be reached in no time at all.

Ruach dances around Jesus and Abba, holding them in her warm wide embrace. It is they who prompted and prodded the Roman authorities until they agreed that the case against Paul's unjust imprisonment should be examined by Caesar himself. It is they who persuaded the authorities to export Paul to Rome on the next available cargo ship.

Oh, how desperately they long for Caesar's heart.

How desperately they long for Caesar to reform his Empire.

Rain lashes down from dark ominous clouds in the centre of Rome. Ruach hovers over the city's imperious sports stadium. The crowds inside are cheering deliriously as two muscular men fight each other with flesh exposed, swords and shields clattering, in a no holds barred battle to the death. Thunder cracks across the skies as the deafening stadium din reaches a crescendo of celebration and the defeated gladiator is decapitated in the name of entertainment.

Ruach cries out in agony.

Grieving the loss of one she loves so dearly; sickened by the violence, so accepted and prevalent; longing and praying for a better world of human dignity and equality.

There is still a long way to go before Jesus' non-violent revolution is complete.

6.05 - Running To Embrace

On the brink of Paul's showdown with Caesar, the narrative on the Headquarters' floor tantalisingly draws to a halt. Did Paul ever receive his chance to speak persuasively about Jesus? It does not say. Phase Six seems to finish incomplete.

A few annotations, however, hint toward the failure of Paul's ambition. Within five years of Paul's arrival, it says that the advocates of Jesus started to experience persecution throughout Rome. In the name of entertainment, Emperor Nero started to burn these 'Christians' at his parties.

And for the next two and a half centuries, persecution persisted.

'Christians' made for excellent entertainment in the Collosseum.

Mauled by gladiators and lions, their deaths were cheered by ecstatic sell-out crowds.

But then.

Quite remarkably.

Perhaps even miraculously.

Our heart is leaping at the revelation.

Emperor Constantine, ruler of the entire Roman Empire, decided to declare himself a 'Christian.' And from that day on, Jesus' radical teachings - where all human lives were precious and valuable - began to gradually transform the Empire's heart.

Change hardly occurred overnight. The annotations point out that for at least the next one hundred years, 'Christian' Emperors continued to sponsor gruesome gladiator battles.

But eventually.

Eventually.

The horrifying gladiator contests were seen as just that: horrifying.

Kneeling on the Headquarters' floor, our eyes open in relief and delight.

This was heaven invading earth.

A new world was being born.

A new creation was blossoming.

'Come, turn around.'

We freeze. The voice is with us, close to us, coming from behind us.

There is no fear within us. We feel totally at peace, completely at ease in our own skin. We are excited, expectant. Moving slowly, like a bride processing down the aisle, we rise and rotate, savouring every second of anticipation.

We fix our eyes upon the feet of a figure five metres away. Tracking upwards, he wears faded navy jeans, his arms are muscular, his chin stubbled, his eyes dark and glistening. Never before have we felt so alive, so at home, so complete, so ecstatic; we are staring into the dark glistening eyes of Jesus.

And without thinking, we are sprinting, sprinting, sprinting, running to embrace.

With arms open wide, Jesus intercepts our stride and swings us round.

Then draws us close.

'Oh, how I've longed for this moment,' he whispers as we bury our head into his safe, secure chest. We are lost in his arms. Time has stopped. There is nowhere else we'd rather be.

We.

Are.

Lost.

In.

The.

Arms.

Of.

Love.

Time returns with a jolt when our right thumb connects with a hole in Jesus' wrist.

Ashamed, our head bows away.

'But... but... but why?' we ask.

Allowing our question to hang, Jesus leads us across to the Phase Five wall, against which he sits, leaning back with feet outstretched. On moving to sit beside him, an image of execution - two perpendicular wooden beams - catches our eye.

'Because *I love you with a love that lasts forever* (Jer. 31:3). Because *the greatest love a person can show is to die for his friends* (John 15:13). Ruach, Abba, and I, we knit you together in an amazing and wonderful way, planning your days before you were born, desiring only the best for you, our child (Ps. 139:14-16). We love you so much it hurts.'

Our eyes close in surrender, allowing Ruach to take hold of Jesus' words and embed them at the very centre of our being. She is surely dancing.

When we open our eyes again, we find Jesus knelt down before our feet holding a wooden bowl, with a towel draped over his shoulder. Jesus removes our shoes and socks. We sit captivated and mystified.

'Ruach, Abba, and I, have been revealing our story of love to you. What you have experienced in this room, that's just the headlines, the highlights. There is so much more for you to discover and discuss.'

Fresh, invigorating water is poured over our tired and dirty feet.

'*The Son of Man did not come to be served. He came to serve others and to give his life as a ransom for many* (Matt. 20:28). *I, your Lord and Teacher, have washed your feet* (John 13:14). Now I invite you to do the same to others. I invite you to play your part in completing Phase Six.'

Jesus rubs our feet back and forth in a simple harmonic motion.

'I have won forgiveness for every one of your friends - love them, serve them and show them the freedom already won for them. Accept others as I have accepted you (Rom. 15:7). Forgive as I have forgiven you.'

We nod, taking it all in. Jesus is wringing out his towel, squeezing every last filthy drip back into the bowl.

'Ruach, Abba and I do *not want anyone to be lost, but* want *all people to change their hearts and lives* (2 Pet. 3:9). *Let your light shine,* so all *may see your good deeds and praise your Father in heaven* (Matt. 5:16). *Be holy because I am holy* (Lev. 19:2).'

'But... but...' we start to protest, taken aback by the extremity of Jesus' words.

'Our breath will help you shine,' Jesus cuts across, realising our fear of inadequacy. 'We understand fully the temptations and struggles in your life. We will be with you, guiding you through it all.'

With our hand in his, Jesus pushes himself up by his knees then helps us to our feet.

'*You can have peace in me. In this world you will have trouble, but be brave! I have defeated the world* (John 16:33).'

As his voice rises climactically, Jesus turns to the Phase Five wall and starts to peel down the posters detailing his resurrection. Hidden beneath, he reveals a dull grey door.

At first we are wooed by a sumptuous perfume, then as the door opens further, a wonderfully kept, diversely coloured garden through which a river flows, visually delights. The complete sensory experience takes our breath away.

'*The Good News about God's Kingdom will be preached in all the world, to every nation. Then the end will come* (Matt. 24:14).'

Jesus turns to us and smiles. He signals for us to follow then steps out into the gorgeously fresh expanse.

'Come, let's go and meet Abba.

'*He will take great delight in you.*

'*He will quiet you with his love.*

'*He will rejoice over you with singing* (Zeph. 3:17*).

'And you will find him with wide open arms, running to embrace.'

PHASE SEVEN

7.00 - Breath Is Stolen

Time plays tricks on you when you reach the age of ninety something. The mind flickers through memories as if they are present realities.

Repulsive.

Haunting.

Spine-chilling memories.

First there's the murder of every one of his friends. Paul was beheaded. Peter was crucified - upside down.

Then there's the demolition of Jerusalem: smoke billowing from smouldering ruins, corpses rotting under rubble. This was the inevitable fate of a city which dared to rise up and challenge the might of the Roman Empire. Jesus predicted that the city's liberation desires would eventually lead to its downfall (Luke 21:24). And so it proved.

Those who tried to flee the annihilation were strung up on the city outskirts. Clothed only in blood, arms swept out across a horizontal wooden beam, legs draped down the vertical, their last breath was stolen from within. The Romans could execute up to five hundred a day.

John's eyes glaze over.

Oh Jesus, beautiful Jesus.

John's suffering may persist, his memories may haunt, but John has no fear.

God's perfect love drives out fear (1 John 4:18).

For *God is love* (1 John 4:16).

And *Love is patient,*

Love is kind.

Love *does not envy.*

It does not boast.

It is not proud.

It is not rude.

It is not self-seeking.

It is not easily angered.

It keeps no record of wrongs…
Love *always protects.*
Always trusts.
Always hopes.
Always perseveres.
Love never fails (1 Cor. 13:7-8*).
John is absolutely besotted, head over heels in love with Love.
Oh, Jesus, sensational Jesus.
There he is, Jesus, the Son of Man travelling on the clouds of heaven (Rev. 1:12).
There he is, eyes blazing like fire, hair *white as snow* (Rev. 1.14).
John's heart is on the brink of explosion. In reality, he is in a dark cave on a remote island. In his mind, he is in heaven.
Wave after wave of sumptuous harmonious singing washes over John; louder than anything John has ever heard before, louder than every person on earth shouting in unison, louder than all the lions roaring.
Lightning flashes, thunder cracks (Rev. 4:5); an emerald coloured rainbow encircles the throne of Elohim (Rev. 4:3); bizarre creatures, of every shape and size, fill the room; yet John's eyes are transfixed upon only one sight.
The sight of one single lamb.
Standing in the centre of Elohim's throne.
The lamb appears slain (Rev. 5:6).
Yet it is clearly alive.
'*Because you were killed,*' the crowds sing, '*with the blood of your death you bought people for God from every tribe, language, people and nation* (Rev. 5:9). *The Lion from the tribe of Judah, David's descendant, has won the victory* (Rev. 5:5).'
John looks on in adoration and awe. He is staring at a defining image of Love - beautiful selfless, self-sacrificing Love. Possessing the power of a lion, Jesus offered himself as a lamb. The image is a rallying cry to those still suffering under the persecution of Emperor Domitian.
To all who endure.
To all who persevere.
To all *who overcome* (Rev. 3:21*).
To all *who win the victory.*
Jesus promises, 'You *will sit with me on my throne* (Rev. 3:21).
'You will have *power over the nations* (Rev. 2:26).

'You will dwell in the *New Jerusalem* (Rev. 3:12).

'You will dwell in the presence of God (Rev. 7:15).

'You *will never be hungry or thirsty again* (Rev. 2:17, 7:16).'

John's mind trips and jolts.

Cheers turn to screams.

Flames rise and engulf.

A burning lake of sulphur stretches out before John's eyes. Its stench is grotesque, putrid, absolutely rancid, and John instantly masks his face, only peering out through his clenched fingers.

From the very beginning of the Rescue Mission, the Hijacker has been crushed on the head (Gen. 3:15), destined for defeat. Yet evil has continued to bite back, clinging to the heel (Gen. 3:15), refusing to let go.

There can be no paradise until all evil is eliminated.

Until all injustice is eradicated.

Until all bloodshed is abolished.

Until all discrimination is demolished.

Majorities must manipulate minorities no more.

Corruption must profit the powerful no more.

All disease must be destroyed.

Death must die (Rev. 20:14).

The Hijacker lets out a searing satanic scream as his clinging grip gives way; and the master of darkness slips and falls *into the lake of burning sulphur.* Flailing in the flames, there he will be *punished day and night for ever and ever* (Rev. 20:10), never to contaminate, capture, conquer, control - never to hijack - a precious human life ever again.

Love, by its very nature, demands justice.

And here, in the burning flames, justice is done.

Howling in agony, the Hijacker reaches out a hand and in one final evil act, grabs hold of a chain of his captives and tugs and pulls them down with him.

Drowning in a cesspit of hatred, Love's precious children:

Breathe.

Out.

For.

The.

Final.

Time.

Tears cascade incessantly from the blood-shot, pain stained eyes of three friends huddled together. Mourning their loss, with arms wrapped around each other, the Community of Elohim weep and grieve with every essence of their being. With their offer of rescue continuously rejected, there is nothing more that can be done.

The lake of fire is the second death (Rev. 20:14). Love's uniquely crafted masterpieces have erased their names from the book of life (Rev. 20:15).

They have rejected life.

They have chosen death.

Writhing in agony, John fights to shut down his mind. He lies rigid on the ground, hands clawing over his eyes, his whole body crying out for all to choose life.

Ruach holds Jesus in a tight intimate embrace. '*Those who win the victory,*' she caresses, '*will not be hurt by the second death* (Rev. 2:11). They *will be dressed in white… I will not erase their names from the book of life* (Rev. 3:5).'

'*I am going to attract her,*' weeps Jesus. '*I will lead her into the desert and speak tenderly to her. There I will give her back her vineyards and I will make the Valley of Trouble a door of hope. There she will respond as when she was young, as when she came out of Egypt. In time, she will call me "my husband"* (Hosea 2:14-16).'

Ruach rises, shimmering with delight. 'Look, my love, w*ho is this coming out of the desert, leaning on her lover? (Song. 8:5)*'

Looking over his shoulder, the Groom's breath is stolen.

Dressed in white *fine linen* (Rev. 19:8) his Bride is gliding gracefully towards him.

She is leaning on the arm of her father.

Leaning on the arm of Abba.

7.01 - Every Desire Is Found

In the beginning the first humans had a choice.
It was a choice between two trees.
One tree
Was called Life.

Fruit from
The other tree
Brought death.

Choose Life...

Choose Life…

Choose Life…

The first humans did not choose Life.

The family of Abraham, the people of Israel were slaves in Egypt.
And as slaves they were hurting.
They were bleeding.
Suffering.
They were crying out in agony.
When Yahweh heard their cries.
And pulled them out of Egypt.
With Moses' help,
Yahweh led them
To the brink
Of paradise.
A land with rivers
And pools of water,
With springs that flow
In the valleys and hills.
With *wheat and barley,*
Vines, fig trees, pomegranates,
Olive oil and honey.
A land with everything

They would ever need (Deut. 8:7-9).

And poised on the brink of paradise
The Israelites were given a choice.
A choice between life and death,
Between blessings and curses.
And Moses begged.
Moses pleaded: '*Now, choose life!* (Deut. 30:19)'

Choose Life...

Choose Life...

Choose Life...

Jesus said, '*I have come*
That they may have life,
And have it to the full (John 10:10*).'
But Jesus was captured.
Jesus was tied to a tree.
And on that tree Jesus hurt.
Jesus bled.
Jesus suffered.
Jesus cried out in agony.
On that tree Jesus died.
...
...
The one who had said he had come to bring life.
...
...
He died.
...
...
...
But after two nights
Of Jesus' dead body
Being buried
In the ground
...
...

Life burst forth from the grave.

Jesus defeated death.
Once and for all.

Leaving Life,
Life in all its fullness,
Reigning victorious.

Jesus *took away the curse* of *the law* (Gal. 3:13).
Now only blessing remains.

Choose Life…

Choose Life…

Choose Life…

Dressed in white *fine linen,*
Bright and clean (Rev. 19:8),
Jesus' Bride glides gracefully towards him.
She is gorgeous and elegant,
Perfectly pure,
Without spot or wrinkle,
Holy and without blemish (Eph. 5:25-27*).

Wrapping his right arm around her waist,
Placing his left hand under her head (Song. 2:6),
Jesus holds his Bride in romantic intimacy.

'*My love, you are full of delights* (Song. 7:6).
My bride, you have thrilled my heart (Song. 4:9).
My bride, your lips drip honey (Song. 4:11).
How beautiful you are, my darling!
Oh, you are beautiful!
Your eyes behind your veil are like doves (Song. 4:1).
My darling, everything about you is beautiful,
There is nothing wrong with you (Song. 4:7).'

'*You are so handsome, my lover* (Song. 1:16).
Your *mouth is sweet to kiss,*
I desire you so *very much.*

You are *my lover and my friend* (Song. 5:16).
You have *brought me to* your *banquet room,*
Your *banner over me is love* (Song. 2:4).
I belong to you *my lover*
And my lover belongs to me (Song. 6:3).
I belong to you *my lover*
And you *desire only me* (Song. 7:10).'

Gazing far into his Bride's eyes,
Jesus tenderly makes his vows:
'My darling, I *will wipe away every tear from* your *eyes.*
There will be no more death,
Or mourning,
Or crying,
Or pain,
For the old order of things has passed away (Rev. 21:4*).
My darling, look, *I am making all things new!* (Rev. 21:5)'

A standing ovation
And deafening applause
Greets the kiss of Husband and Wife
As a *new Jerusalem* comes *down*
Out of heaven from God (Rev. 21:2).

'*Arise, my darling, my beautiful one,*
And come with me (Song. 2:10*).
Look, the winter is past;
The rains are over and gone.
Blossoms appear through all the land.
The time has come to sing;
The cooing of doves is heard in our land (Song. 2:11-12).'

Walking hand in hand,
Husband and Wife step
Into a panorama of paradise.
Every flower is in bloom.
Every crop bears fruit.
Every creature lives in harmony.

Even *wolves and lambs eat together in peace* (Is. 65:25).

Here in paradise,
Husband and Wife
Dwell forever
In intimacy together.

Full of joy, there is no pain.
Full of love, there is no shame.
Full of Life, there is no Death.

The first humans were born
Into a similar paradise.
Sharing the creative character of their creator,
Humans chose to build onto the lush green landscape.
                    Some constructions were oppressive.
                            Stifling and damaging.
                    Others were objects of beauty.
                    Others brought order and structure.
                    Huge cities emerged,
                    Enabling large populations
                    To live together in community.
                This was progress.
            Advancement.
And here in the new creation,
Elohim takes the work of human hands,
And transforms it into paradise.

The new creation contains a city,
Decorated with every kind of jewel (Rev. 21:19).
Emeralds, sapphires, pearls: New Jerusalem has them all.
The street is *made of pure gold as clear as glass* (Rev. 21:21).
Husband and Wife stand overwhelmed by the majesty.
The city gates are named after Israel's twelve tribes (Rev. 21:12).
Its foundation stones named after Jesus' twelve closest disciples (Rev. 21:14).

In New Jerusalem,
Every covenant finds fulfilment.
The new creation begun with Noah,
The blessing of all people, promised to Abraham,
The full blessing of the law presented to Moses,
The everlasting kingdom, ruled by the descendant of David,
It is all present, all made possible,
By the blood of Jesus' new covenant (2 Cor. 1:20).

In New Jerusalem,
There is no need for a Temple.
Yahweh's Shekinah is everywhere.
God's presence is with his people (Rev. 21:3).
Ruach inhabits every life.

In New Jerusalem,
The sun is superfluous.
The glory of God is its light (Rev. 21:23).

In New Jerusalem,
It will never be night again (Rev. 22:5).
God is light, and in him there is no darkness (1 John 1:5).

Lost in each other's arms,
Husband and Wife walk beside the river,
Flowing down from the throne of God.
The river is *shining like crystals.*
It contains *the water of life* (Rev. 22:1).

Jesus dips his hand into the water.
'Let whoever is thirsty come,' he ushers.
'I will give free water … to those who win the victory (Rev. 21:6-7).
'Whoever wishes may have the water of life as a free gift (Rev. 22:17).'

Whoever wishes may win.
Love has paid the price.
Victory is free.
All can choose life.

'To those who win the victory,'
Declares Jesus, radiant with joy,
'I will give the right to eat the fruit
From the tree of life (Rev. 2:7*).'

In the beginning the first humans had a choice.
It was a choice between two trees.

In New Jerusalem,
There is only one tree.
Life: it has been chosen.

Abba takes the hand of Jesus on his right and Ruach on his left.
Locked in embrace, the view electrifies Elohim's heart.
Everywhere they look, their every desire is found.
With justice realised, their character surrounds.
With beauty restored, their creativity abounds.
With intimacy chosen, relationship resounds.
Love beams with a great satisfied smile.
The Rescue Mission is complete.

Special thanks to Rachel Helen Smith
for her tireless encouragements and proof-reading.

Cover design: www.annieliggins.com

Pete Atkinson is a qualified teacher.
He has a Masters degree from Cambridge University.

The Rescue Mission is his first book.